"Another magnificent and awesome book by the inventor of ***Quantum Field Psychology***, Dr. Dalrymple, who has brilliantly used various kinds of mathematics in order to formulate and expound the structure of his theory. He has managed to describe and illustrate his theory in a way that is clear and intelligible. For anyone who is seeking to use math to describe the complicated and emotional relationships among all human beings, I certainly recommend this book."

Michael A. Tisher, M.A., ABD
Associate Professor of Mathematics, University of Maryland University College, Asian Division

"Dr. Dalrymple, in his fascinating book, ***Quantum Field Psychology***, *The Thoton Particle Theory*, raises the field of psychology to a new plane - one where hard science resides! By deconstructing emotions in the systematic, logical language of physics - he reveals emotions as measurable and tangible - a truly amazing scientific breakthrough."

Katina Matthews-Ferrari, M.D.
Adjunct Professor of Psychiatry
University of Florida, Gainesville, Florida

QUANTUM FIELD PSYCHOLOGY
The Thoton Particle Theory

Second Edition

by

Ron Dalrymple, Ph.D.
Associate Professor
University of Maryland - European
Division

Copyright Dr. Ron Dalrymple 2018

Celestial Gifts Publishing
POB 4466
N. Ft. Myers, FL
33918

QUANTUM FIELD PSYCHOLOGY
THE THOTON PARTICLE THEORY

Ron Dalrymple, Ph.D.
Second Edition

Published by:
Celestial Gifts Publishing
Post Office Box 4466
N. Ft. Myers, FL 33918   U.S.A.
drrondal@hotmail.com

Copyright Information

Quantum Field Psychology

The Thoton Particle Theory

Second Edition

Includes bibliographical references.

((Topical Headings:

1.) Psychology

2.) Mathematical models

3.) Quantum field theory and psychology.

4.) Thought and thinking - mathematical models.

5.) Topology and quantum thinking.

6.) New scientific theory.

7.) New paradigm of thought.

First Edition, 2004
© Copyright 2004 Dr. Ron Dalrymple
ISBN: 9781530567294

Second Edition, 2018
© Copyright 2018 Dr. Ron Dalrymple
ISBN - 13: 978-1727740318
ISBN - 10: 1727740319

Publisher's Cataloging-In-Publication Data
(Prepared by The Donohue Group, Inc.)

Names: Dalrymple, Ron, author.
Title: Quantum field psychology : the thoton particle theory / Ron Dalrymple, Ph.D., Associate Professor, University of Maryland - European Division.

Description: Second edition. | N. Ft. Myers, FL : Celestial Gifts Publishing, [2018] | Includes bibliographical references.

Identifiers: ISBN 9781727740318 | ISBN 1727740319
Subjects: LCSH: Psychology--Mathematical models. | Quantum field theory and psychology. | Thought and thinking--Mathematical models.

Classification: LCC BF39 .D29 2018 | DDC 150.72--dc23

ABOUT THE AUTHOR

Dr. Ron Dalrymple has been a licensed psychologist in Maryland, Pennsylvania, Missouri, Kansas, Arkansas, Colorado, Idaho, Florida, Arizona and New Zealand, with a special interest in the higher, seldom understood powers of the mind. He received his Ph.D. in psychology from the University of Maryland in 1984.

Combining years of clinical experience with research in physics, topological mathematics and philosophical analyses of Eastern and Western origins, he devised a meta-theoretical system of thought now expressed as Quantum Field Psychology.

He is a member of Mensa, is a Diplomate in Forensic Psychology, belongs to numerous psychological associations and is listed in Who's Who in America, Who's Who in Editors, Writers and Poets, Who's Who in the East, Who's Who in the World, and Who's Who in U.S. Authors and Writers.

He wrote a newspaper column for five years titled "*The Voice Within,*" and did a radio talk show in Maryland by the same title.

His motivational books include **The Inner Manager**, **8 Days to Creative Power**, **I Love You, God**, and **Quantum Field Psychology**, listed elsewhere in this publication, all best-sellers.

He produced a best-selling film about the discovery of Quantum Field Psychology, **Paradise Found 2015,** and his new two hour documentary, **The Endless Question,** is scheduled for release in 2019.

All of his works are found on Amazon.com.

WARNING - DISCLAIMER

This book is designed to provide information and creative ideas relative to the subject matter covered. It is sold with the understanding that the publisher and author are not engaged in rendering professional psychological services or consulting services of any kind.

If professional psychological or other services are required, a competent professional should be sought.

It is not the purpose of this book to reprint or represent all the information or ideas pertaining to this subject matter, but rather complement, amplify and supplement other texts. For more information see References or consult other sources.

This book can be used as a source of stimulation and insight, but not as the ultimate resource on psychological procedures, concepts or issues.

Other resources will present radically different views, and this work is in no way intended to usurp or contradict those divergent points of view.

The purpose of this book is to educate and entertain. The author and publisher shall have neither liability nor responsibility to any person or entity with respect to any loss or damage caused or alleged to be caused directly or indirectly by the informatIon and ideas contained in this book.

WARNING - DISCLAIMER

Disclaimer

The publisher assumes no responsibility for the use or misuse of this product, or for any injury, damage and/or financial loss alleged or sustained to persons or property as a result of using this report. This book is presented as an inspirational axiomatic theory, and is not to be interpreted or utilized as psychological advice or direction in any form. If such is sought, the individual might seek the assistance of a mental health professional.

The publishers cannot guarantee your future results and/or success in any venue, as there are unknown risks and factors in any business or personal venture. The use of this information should be based on your own due diligence and free will, and you agree that neither the publisher nor employees or staff are liable in any form for any success or failure of your personal behavior, experiences or business, that is directly or indirectly related or alleged to be related to the purchase and/or use of this book.

If you cannot abide by this agreement, you can return the first copy of the product purchased to the publisher for a full refund.
Thank-you.

Abstract

This paper is a theoretical consideration of the application of quantum physics and topological mathematics to the human mind as an energy field, a concept first hypothesized by the author in 1969.

It is axiomatically postulated that the mind extends beyond the human brain, and that the functions of the mind can be described mathematically.

Applications are drawn to the functions of thought, emotion, personality structure and human communication.

Implications of this framework include a theoretical basis from which to reformulate current modes of psychological investigation and analysis, with the potential for integrating the disparate approaches of physical and social sciences into one.

TABLE OF CONTENTS

Introduction   20

Axioms of Quantum Field Psychology:
Axiom 1   51

Axiom 2. THOT/EMOT waves manifest
as sinusoidal FOURIER WAVES   57

Axiom 3: Dalrymple's Law   62

Axiom 4: Transverse Waves   67

Axiom 5: Gradients of Thought   68

Axiom 5, Lemma 3: Psychological Defense
Mechanisms

Axiom 5, Lemma 6: Mood Disorders   74

Axiom 6: Thoton Particle   82

Axiom 6, Lemma 8: The Ego   89

Axiom 7: Energy Fields   90

Axiom 7, Lemma 2: Superconscious Mind   91

Axiom 7, Lemma 3: Chakras   91

Axiom 7, Lemma 4: Subconscious Mind   94

Axiom 7, Lemma 10: Cognitive Schema   97

Axiom 7, Lemma 11: Dissociative Disorders   97

Axiom 7, Lemma 12: Mathematics of Mental Space   98

Axiom 7, Lemma 13: Topology   100

Axiom 8: Personality Disorders   103

Axiom 9: Human Relationships   134

Axiom 10: Consciousness   138

Axiom 10, Lemma 5: Quantum Fields   141

Axiom 10, Lemma 6: Superconsciousness   142

Axiom 10, Lemma 8: Manifestation   143

Axiom 11: Planetary Consciousness   144

Axiom 12: Training   146

Conclusions   148

References   150

Other Books by Dr. Ron Dalrymple   158

Introduction

The history of psychological theory has gone through stages.

Just as we have stage theories, we have ***theory stages***, stemming from numerous psychological and scientific roots. Each of these roots reflects their times, each theory a projection of the beliefs and approaches to knowledge entertained by the extant scientific community of that age.

Some of these beliefs reflect particles of truth, others are rudimentary reflections spawned from the insights, misperceptions and even delusions of their creators. These biases at times illuminate, and at times obfuscate the scientific community's perceptions and belief systems.

Kuhn (1966, p. 4) discussed, "An apparently arbitrary element, compounded of personal and historical accident, is always a formative ingredient of the beliefs espoused by a given scientific community at a given time."

Such is the nature of progress, a meandering circumlocution of partial truths which at times puncture the facades of the day, and at times are **entrained** by them.

Many belief systems are patterned by paradigm. Kuhn (1966 p. 3) observes there exists an, "...insufficiency of methodological directives, by themselves, to dictate a unique substantive conclusion to many sorts of scientific questions."

As Hamlet remarked, "There are more things in Heaven and Hell, Horatio, than meet thy philosophy."

Many approaches are entrained by **sensory-centric belief systems**, the ordination of sensory processes as the supreme source of knowledge and therefore the only reliable and valid methodology. Others attempt to go beyond this systematology.

When Aristotle departed from the ways of Socrates and Plato, he left the tradition of deductive logic and abstract argument. Against the tides of his day, he emphasized observation and classification of nature.

He created the first Organon, an attempt to make sense out of the world (Ouspensky, 1981, p. 221). He set the foundation for the scientific method and established The Lyceum, a rival school to Plato's Academy (Myers, 2004, p. 2).

What is most important is Aristotle's quantum leap to a new level of analysis, a new way of approaching nature which laid the foundation for many sciences. This constituted a paradigm shift.

When Bacon proposed the **<u>Novum Organum</u>** in 1602, he began where Aristotle left off and added essential components of what became the modern scientific method (Ouspensky, 1981, p. 221). He advocated the observation of nature, the collection of data, and the use of the inductive method to abstract theories from observation (Smith & Davis, 2003, p. 42).

Once theories are generated, hypotheses can be drawn and tested deductively. The powerful combination of observation, the objective collection of data and the dual use of induction and deduction has unveiled to humankind much information about the physical world.

Like Aristotle, Bacon leapt to a new level of thought with profound consequences. A paradigm shift that restructured the world.

However, the method is limited to the physical senses and thereby precludes investigation of the vast majority of the universe. The physical senses and our instrumentation at this point in time allows us to perceive but a minute portion of the vibratory range of energies that abound in the universe.

Pertaining to light energy alone (Flanagan, 1997), we are only aware of less than 0.01% of the total available light that surrounds us.

A new paradigm shift is needed to go beyond this model, which gave rise to Ouspensky's (1981) work.

Each of the aforementioned paradigm shifts was of a metatheoretical nature, because they took the theories, conjectures, misperceptions and half-truths of the day and leapt beyond them to a whole new way of thinking.

These societal quantum leaps are mimicked by the individual evolving child in Piaget's (1976) theory, with the child acquiring a new systematology of thought and analysis with each jump to a new level of cognitive functioning.

The sensorimotor level is a naming stage, with the child orienting to the world and labeling objects and people. The child begins to evolve a sense of self versus other. Aristotle brought early science to this level, creating the foundation for what followed. He extensively classified nature, a necessary first step in studying it.

During Piagetian pre-operations, the child begins one-dimensional thought, learning to order objects and rank them along a specific dimension. Many followers of Aristotle functioned at this level for centuries after his death, debating various issues as they were guided by his genius - but limited by the model given.

In concrete operations, the child can perform two-dimensional thought, co-varying two dimensions at once, such as shape versus size. This is the level proposed by Bacon, where other factors are held constant (ideally) so that specific variables can be observed interacting.

This model quickly evolves into working with 3 or more variables, via various experimental designs. And in formal operations, the child can co-vary 3 or more dimensions at once, truly performing abstract thought. Here, the powers of the imagination exponentiate.

The world of modern science has remained at the level of formal operations for the last four hundred years.

Ouspensky (1981, p. 226) created **Tertium Organum** to postulate a world of cause beyond the physical world, a world where mind is supreme, where time is spatial, where causes and consequences exist simultaneously.

The world of science has done little to comprehend or absorb these concepts. Instead, other lines of development have been followed, primarily the sensory-centric model.

Exemplifying this line of development, and on the opposite end of the spectrum of Ouspensky, Wundt began with an intent to investigate the mind, searching for the atoms of consciousness.

He lacked systematology adequate to lend credibility to either his technique of *introspection*, or to his methodology. But he did begin experimental psychology in 1879 at Leipzig, Germany, a monumental undertaking.

Wundt's student Titchener brought introspection to the USA in the form of structuralism, which eventually eroded in the face of American pragmatism and other approaches.

William James of Harvard did much to advent psychology, with ***The Principles of Psychology***, a 1400-page work published in 1890, still venerated today. His American pragmatism rang out, but did not present a unified theory.

Freud developed a theory-based system of treatment subsequent to his $N = 1$ studies, framing his theory in part on 17th century mechanics developed by Newton.

Using a closed, 3-dimensional system of cause and effect, Freud evolved a productive set of concepts which have spurred many other theoretical and therapeutic approaches, despite having fallen under much criticism by dissenting practitioners and academics both in his time and today.

Given the vagaries of psychoanalysis and introspection to move beyond the speculative, Pavlov's work gave birth to Watson, and Thorndike to Skinner. Behaviorism produced much new research on learning and dominated American psychology for decades.

Radical behaviorism proffered a strict adherence to observation and experimentation, the epitome of sensory-centric analyses.

Computer technology began to explode in the 1960s, leading to much current research in information processing, fueling the cognitive revolution.

These influences helped evolve cognitive behavior modification and other therapeutic perspectives, which reactivated Wundt and his consideration of the atoms of consciousness. Thought-emotion-behavior cycles and other perspectives are now broadly entertained by therapists.

Much social science research is now based on the use of statistics, which has evolved in part for lack of more reliable and valid approaches.

Assumptions are made about sample populations when statistics are used, assumptions which may not be met.

For example, we assume homoscedasticity, that equal variances apply to samples compared, when this assumption is often violated. Even worse, we do not know when it is violated, leaving many of our conclusions in research specious at best.

It is like searching for a lost object on a street corner that has a light, when we lost the object on a different corner, in the dark.

Each approach has contributed toward an increasing body of knowledge and understanding, but none has put together an overall theory adequate to explain, predict and understand the entire field of psychology.

Moreover, since our senses function within a 3-dimensional space, with a fourth dimension when we add time, our sciences and beliefs have evolved in concert with this limited systematology. We see what we believe, and we theorize what we experience.

Recognizing the inadequacy of any 3 or 4-dimensional, cause-effect system in psychology to explain, predict or fully understand human thought, emotion and behavior, Ouspensky (1981) postulated his Tertium Organum, adding the element of mind to the equation.

Many other systems of transpersonal contemplation have been posited since, although none have proffered a formulation that sufficiently integrates hard sciences with social sciences, nor eastern with western philosophies of the mind to a degree that would constitute a unified field theory.

Each of these prior theories reflect their times and technology and are projections of their creator's comprehension of the world of their time. None explains all the variance of the universe, allows perfect prediction or perfect replication.

Many theorists have called for this (Wilbur, 2003, p. 45), recognizing a need for an integral theory to explain consciousness and the universe at large. We know that the best theory explains the most variance, is parsimonious, allows prediction and replication (Smith & Davis, 2003, p. 201).

What is most striking is that Einstein introduced his Special Theory of Relativity in 1905 (Herbert, 1985 p. 7), and yet his work has been ignored or completely misunderstood by the majority of other sciences beyond the world of quantum physics.

Most sciences today are predicated upon a Newtonian, 3-dimensional framework, limiting perspectives of thought and research paradigms.

It is suggested that a broader perspective is needed to integrate a diversity of investigative approaches. When we integrate Einstein, Planck, Schroedinger, Bohn and others, we are availed of a much broader perspective than previously posited by psychological theory.

The intent of Quantum Field Psychology is to propose a holistic theory designed to integrate physical with social sciences and Eastern with Western traditions.

Psychological theory might be described as mathematics sculpted with poetry. We need a sound foundation of scientific premise and fact, woven together with the beauty and intricacies of human creativity, the intuitive leaps and insights observed by Kuhn (1966).

What is proposed is a paradigm shift, moving to a meta-formal operations level, where n-dimensions are **covaried** at once in our analysis. This constitutes a *tensor field*, where every variable affects every other variable simultaneously in the universe.

The author was researching these issues while teaching college in Sicily, where Archimedes lived and worked. He came across an ancient fable. An admirer of Archimedes, Gnosius, had been investigating the nature of fire, wanting to discover the source of its heat and light.

Gnosius traveled about the Mediterranean by ship, searching for answers. Little had been learned of this mysterious force, and as he looked far and wide he discovered by accident a team of investigators who called themselves, *"smoke-eaters."*

For an entire century, they had followed the preambles of their founder, Ignatius, who had institutionalized a method of tasting, snorting and dancing through smoke.

They would build huge bonfires by the Mediterranean at night and dance naked over the embers, rubbing themselves in charcoal and howling at the moon.

Each luminary of the group would take his turn, after their nocturnal cavortings, giving dissertations on his particular spin about smoke.

Unable to directly access the true nature of fire, each had a pet theory about what they could see, smell and taste...smoke.

One called himself a **"radical smoke-eater,"** insisting that only smoke that could be tasted and smelled should be investigated. After all, if the senses couldn't indulge it, how could it be of merit for consideration by other smoke-eaters?

He railed against his competitors, who foolishly insisted on sampling smoke of little taste or color, and therefore of little merit. He dismissed them as primitive and inconsequential.

Another called himself an **"action smoke-eater,"** because he insisted on studying the actions of smoke as it was carried by the wind. He plotted countless meanderings of the smoke over time, insisting he was making progress and was approaching a major breakthrough.

None came.

He spent years drawing graphs in the sand, each washed away by a new tide or storm, each drawn again and again by his endless actions.

Another theorist interrogated all consumers of smoke with endless questions, such as, "How does the smoke make you feel? How old were you when you first smelled smoke?"

He ran groups for young smoke-eaters, and got them to share their feelings. Many spoke of how much they had grown from the experience.

Each of the professors would make huge inscriptions of his theories in the sand, and they would argue for days over who was right and who was wrong, at times coming to fist fights.

One of the elders of the group, Pontius, insisted he was the true genius among them. He would strut and parade with great ceremony, pontificating on who should be venerated, and who should be expelled from the inner circle of deserved genius.

Annually, Pontius held ceremonies and gave awards for the past year's most prestigious work, awards carved from driftwood. The recipients would place the awards in their huts by the fire, and at nighttime, in secret, would bow to the awards, groveling and rolling in the darkened sand.

Some would chant and make elaborate signs, supplicating themselves to their own egos. Pontius smiled at all this. None of them, he secretly confided, could ever challenge him. Time passed, and he gave way to old age and too much wine. He became feeble, but could still occasionally deliver a fiery oration.

He eventually died, content that his work had changed the world forever. Generations passed, with smoke-eaters groups having sprung up all over the Mediterranean.

One day, the group was interrupted during a monologue by Ignatius IV, the descendant of their great founder. The obese Ignatius was strutting in front of his seated spectators, many of whom yawned and traded knowing glances.

Suddenly, one of them leapt up and gave a shout. A man was swimming ashore, torn and beaten by the sea. He was in tattered clothes and was barely alive. He stumbled toward them and collapsed on the sand.

It was Gnosius.

As they rushed to him, he lifted a hand, barely able to speak. "I am Gnosius...my ship...sank...all hands lost." Exhausted from his struggle with death, he collapsed. It took him many days to recover.

He had long hair and a beard, and they marveled at him. Many whispered, "Who is this strange invader, and what are his intentions?"

As Gnosius slowly recovered, he would sit by the fire, listening to the endless harangues. When he finally regained the strength to stand and talk, he spoke to them with a voice resonant with humility.

"I thank you all for helping me, now perhaps I can help you."

Ignatius stood and bowed, "We smoke-eaters, the intellectuals of this land, welcome you. But...how could you help us?"

Muffled laughter suffused the crowd. Many smirked and traded knowing looks.

Gnosius smiled faintly and bowed. "I do not wish to interject any dissension into your fine proceedings, but...there is another way of looking at this phenomena."

"Oh?" rang out Ignatius, his voice arch. He stood slowly, leaning on his cane.

"Yes, you see, I am what is called a scientist in my land, a natural philosopher. In a humble way, our job is to understand and explain nature, as do all of you."

Ignatius' nose climbed into the air. Others imitated him, some choking on their phlegm.

Gnosius continued, "If I may be so bold, it seems your investigations of smoke are missing the point. Why not investigate fire itself?"

Shocked, Ignatius clutched at his chest, his eyes wild with horror. He pumped at the air, then fell backward into the sand.

The entire congregation leapt up and began kicking sand at Gnosius, shouting, "Sacrilege! Kill him! Kill the infidel!"

Others began to throw rocks.

Ducking, Gnosius raised his hands for order. "Please friends, what danger is there in trying to see another point of view? Perhaps even revamping your entire philosophy?"

He winced from the pummeling.

Ignatius howled. "What danger? We are the scribes of our world, we are the authority! How dare you question us?"

They charged at him and he dove back into the sea.

Gnosius swam all night, until he found another island where he eventually founded a new temple of thought.

He later returned to Siracusa, Sicily, where he and Archimedes took to the baths and howled in laughter at his exploits.

To all the smoke-eaters of the world we dedicate this new theory.

When Faraday (Guillen, 1995) was rebuked by the Royal Academy...

When Daniel Bernoulli had his ideas usurped by his own father...

When Einstein turned the world on its head…

When Tesla changed the world with his inventions and was robbed and defiled by corporate parasites…

To all of these, this work is dedicated, a turning on its head of psychology and psychiatry. Rather than drawing upon a 3- or 4- or even 5- dimensional framework, this theory is predicated upon n-dimensional fields of high energy physics.

Capra's (2000, p. 303) original work, **<u>The Tao of Physics</u>**, first published in 1975, observed, "...the significance of the parallels between the world views of physicists and mystics is beyond any doubt. The interesting question, then, is not whether these parallels exist, but why; and, furthermore, what their existence implies."

It is one intent of quantum field psychology to humbly propose an answer to this question.

The essence of the scientific method is to maintain an open mind, and to assume nothing. Yet egos become entranced by their own creations, mesmerized into ignoring or discounting competing evidence.

Jung (1963, p. 155-156) elicited this phenomena when meeting with Freud in Vienna in 1909. He recounts asking Freud what he thought of precognition and parapsychology.

"Because of his materialistic prejudice, he rejected this entire complex of questions as nonsensical, and did so in terms of so shallow a positivism that I had difficulty in checking the sharp retort on the tip of my tongue."

The arrogance and narcissism of materialistic viewpoints is legendary. We observed that psychological theory has been dominated for centuries by **sensory-centric** formulations.

In contrast, Quantum Field Psychology is a mathematically-based, **thought-centric theory** that integrates psychology with physics and proposes a methodology to be followed in further investigations.

It attempts to integrate the implications of many disparate approaches to understanding the nature of the human mind and its functions.

In order to achieve this, we have incorporated the findings of less traditional investigations conducted in the Soviet Union and Eastern Block countries over the last many decades.

The **assimilation** (Piaget, 1976) of more traditional approaches to psychology brings us to a point of impedance, where only the **accommodation** of our precepts into broader perspectives allows us to transcend the earlier constructs.

When Ostander and Schroeder (1970) published their seminal work on research behind the Iron Curtain on the psychic functions of mind, it was variously received with awe, skepticism, anger and rebuke.

Efforts of Soviets to find **"laws of mind"** were invoked (Ostander & Schroeder, 1970, p. 4), where the functions of the human mind can be described as part of natural science, little understood throughout history.

These researchers report that in 1966 (Ostander & Schroeder, 1970, p. 5), Karl Nikolaiev sat in Leningrad and received Morse code sent telepathically from Moscow. Shifts in his brain wave patterns were recorded, with an attempt to resolve these into words.

The Soviet perspective (Stander & Schroeder, 1970, p. 8) is that telepathy influences all situations, with minds interacting continuously to contribute to perceptions, feelings and thoughts within a group. They further hypothesize that some people like, and others instantly dislike each other due to these factors.

This source of energy would also interact between groups, with the size of influence being a function of energy projected, emotional intensity, clarity of mental-emotional focus, duration of concentration and perhaps a host of other factors.

Support for this premise is found in the work of Emoto (2004), where beautiful and loving thoughts manifest harmonious crystalline structures in water, and negative, inharmonious thoughts manifest mishappen and distorted formations. Since humans are largely water, the implications of Emoto's work are profound.

Nikolaiev (Ostander & Schroeder, 1970, p. 14) stated the sender is equally important in telepathy. If the sender's thoughts are hazy, the receiver will get foggy pictures.

The sender in Nikolaiev's experiment visualized the object to be sent telepathically, then visualized the receiver and imagined looking at the object through the receiver's eyes.

In other studies involving Ms. Mikhail-ova (Ostander & Schroeder, 1970, p. 76), scientist Edward Naumov opined that the negative projections of skeptical scientists observing her attempts to perform psychokinesis might delay her efforts for hours.

However, she would still manifest the feat to be performed. With supportive observers, he stated, she might move an object within minutes.

Engineer Victor Popovkin (Ostander & Schroeder, 1970, p. 15), opined that all people have this ability, and it can be trained and developed in all.

Attempts to track Nikolaiev's brain wave patterns while performing telepathy (Ostander & Schroeder, 1970, p. 21-22) revealed an alpha rhythm at the beginning of his efforts, and activation of the occipital lobe as if he were receiving visual information, and the temporal region as if he were receiving auditory information. Both forms of input paralleled brain functions in these areas as if he was receiving physical stimuli.

Perhaps more interesting is the report that EEG patterns would signal his receiving the telepathically sent information, whether he was consciously aware of it or not (Ostander & Schroeder, 1970, p. 21-22).

Does this support the contention that the brain is constantly receiving telepathic information, but the conscious mind for most people is trained to block it out?

Naumov (Ostander & Schroeder, 1970, p. 28) stated much research supported the contention that emotions are also projected from mind to mind, and that powerful, spontaneous emotional outbursts are transmitted perhaps all the more effectively.

Is this a survival mechanism, developed powerfully in our ancestors, now partially lost due to a change in society? We now rely less on such functions for survival since we live in concrete jungles, not prehistoric ones.

A study referenced (In Ostander & Schroeder, 1970, p. 29) completed by Duane & Behrendt (1965), showed that if one identical twin entered the alpha state, the other twin would as well, despite being at a distance.

Naumov (Ostander & Schroeder, 1970, p. 31-3) reported having found that in 65% of their cases investigated, there was a strong telepathic bond between mother and child.

He further described spontaneous sympathy pains during surgeries between family members at great distances, and flashes of telepathy occurring most often between family members, people in love and childhood friends.

Mother rabbit's brains react when their children are being killed at a distance, and Backster (In Ostander & Schroeder, 1970, p. 33) found that plants react when shrimp are being killed in the area.

Kamensky (Ostander & Schroeder, 1970, p. 34-5) found that negative emotions being blasted from one person to another would fatigue the receiver, with an EEG that shifted into delta and theta waves.

The receivers also experienced unpleasant body sensations and strong head pains. The receiver's EEG normalized within one to three minutes, once the sender began projecting calm, positive emotions to the receiver.

In 1956, Drs. Serov and Troskin (In Winn, R., Ed., 1961) found the number of white blood cells rose by fifteen hundred after they suggested positive emotions to patients. After impressing negative emotions, the white blood cells decreased by sixteen hundred.

If these findings should prove to be reliable, valid and replicable, the implications coincide with the posits of Quantum Field Psychology.

One quest of Quantum Field Psychology is to use mathematical models and quantum physics to integrate biological science with quantum physics, psychological theory and psychical research, in an attempt to create a **unified field theory**.

There is an ancient expression that states, "As above, so below. As within, so without."

May this humble integration of axiomatic mathematical models inspire more research into the essence of the fire within. We have been breathing smoke long enough.

LEGEND: For the sake of simplicity in mathematical expressions, thought is abbreviated as THOT, and emotion as EMOT. THOT/EMOT is also abbreviated as T/E.

AXIOMS OF QUANTUM FIELD PSYCHOLOGY

AXIOM 1. THOT/EMOT waves are generated by the mind as an interaction of biological, sensory, perceptual, memory and abstracting processes, which transcend and project beyond the human brain. Every human THOT/EMOT generates its corresponding pilot wave, which travels through space.

The pilot wave parallels deBroglie's proposal in 1924 that a pilot wave is attached to every particle of matter. DeBroglie's concept was quickly adopted by Einstein (Herbert, 1985, p. 40).

The emanation of waveforms from living organisms provides an explanation for ESP phenomena, plant reactions to thought, animals that respond to human emotion and mental states, and many other phenomena found by Soviet and former Eastern block countries chronicled by Ostander and Schroeder (1970).

Rodriquez et al (1999), may have found support for the neuronal basis of thought waves with their finding that, after distributed parts of the brain do their processing, for 1/4th of a second, thousands of neurons emit equivalent signals at 40 times per second, creating gamma waves.

This may underlie **the binding problem** (Pinel, 2004), the question of how the parallel processing of information in different brain areas is reintegrated into the holographs we see in consciousness.

Neural synchrony may form the basis of consciousness, giving a continuously changing focus that constitutes the "perceptual now," the internal movie screen of attention.

Wolf Singer (Coren et al, 2004. p. 339) found further support for neuronal synchrony with the discovery that active neurons have a tendency to cause other neurons with which they are connected to fire with precisely the same temporal pattern on a millisecond scale. Participants in this research wore caps of electrodes registering **ERPs**, event-related potentials.

Neural synchrony shows firing coincidences which seem to increase and decrease in cycles, creating waves of activation that repeat themselves between 20 and 60 times a second.

These oscillations take the form of Fourier waves, and may reveal that different brain areas are in communication about the same visual object (Coren et al, 2004. p. 339).

This may be the substrate of how varying patterns are produced in consciousness, where different cortical areas firing in a vast array of patterns produce an abundance of conscious domains.

Edelman (1987) formulated the concept of neural Darwinism, in that some cortical connections survive and flourish, and others become extinct.

He also introduced the idea of re-entrant neural processing, or neural feedback loops in the processing of consciousness.

Edelman and Tononi (2000) built upon these concepts in their discussion of the dynamic core of consciousness, where synchronous activity of neurons in different brain regions is both necessary and sufficient for perceptual awareness to occur.

Perceptual objects currently in consciousness at any given time are represented by the dynamic core, and those not so represented are not currently in consciousness.

For vision, this means synchronous time-locking occurs between dorsal and ventral streams, the thalamus, amygdala and the frontal and parietal lobes. Rees et al. (2002) built upon this concept in proposing a need for synchrony to occur at some level of strength for consciousness to occur.

LEMMA 1. THOT/EMOT waves are enzymatic both within the human body and throughout the environment of the individual. THOT/EMOT elements spark the actions of other T/E components, as well as physiological processes and material functions and forms in the environment.

LEMMA 2. THOT/EMOT waves are concentrated in focus and effect by holding the conscious attention fixed upon specific cognitive imagery with a specific emotional current.

LEMMA 3. If THOT/EMOT waves are not concentrated, then the probability of any specific combination of frequencies being projected is determined by a stochastic process (Larson, 1969, p. 122) embracing probabilities expressed by:

$$P(x,k) = \frac{x^k \bullet e^{-x}}{k!} \quad , k = 0, 1, 2..... \text{ or perhaps}$$

$$P(x,k,{}^{\wedge}s) = \frac{({}^{\wedge}s)^k \bullet e^{-({}^{\wedge}s)}}{k!} \quad , k = 0, 1, 2.......$$

giving a Poisson random variable x with parameter $\wedge s$, where the Poisson process $\wedge$ is observed for s units of time.

The Poisson process state is approached most closely by a mind totally unfocused, where any given THOT/EMOT complex has an equal chance of occurring.

This never actually transpires since THOT/EMOT complexes help to compel specific forms to manifest. The Poisson state is a limit toward which a disintegrating mind approaches.

E. g., drugs, alcohol and negative thinking may precipitate decompensation.

LEMMA 4. As the THOT/EMOT wave varies as a function of slight or greater perturbations, a FAMILY OF FREQUENCIES may be engendered.

This produces variations of the originally intended form to crystallize.

AXIOM 2. THOT/EMOT waves manifest as sinusoidal **FOURIER WAVES**, expressed as:

$w = kap(1)+ ...+ kap(n)$; where w = wave form; k = spatial frequency, or the frequency that occurs within a specific distance; a = amplitude; p = phase.

Each complex THOT/EMOT can therefore be broken into component sine wave frequencies and analyzed as to the specific elements which contribute to its creation.

Any given THOT/EMOT may be a composite of numerous unconscious, preconscious and conscious contributory thoughts and feelings.

The composite of wave forms creates a THOT/EMOT field of energy around the individual, which interacts with all other energy fields on a continuous basis.

Each component *kap(i)* can combine with other *kap(j)* components to magnify waveform effects, or to partially or completely cancel each other out.

A ***tensor field*** is created, where every particle of matter and energy interacts with every other particle throughout the universe on a continuous basis.

The mind is therefore a tensor field, as is the entire universe. Since all tensor fields continuously interact, each human mind is in continuous contact with the entire universe.

Some of the *kap(i)* are static, or more or less constant in the frequency (f) which they emanate. Other *kap(i)* are dynamic, much more fluid in frequency range, amplitude and periodicity, and in many cases a more transitory resident of consciousness.

LEMMA 1. Some THOT/EMOT waves occur as impulse waves, especially those predicated upon fear and other negative emotions. These manifest as:

THOT-EMOT

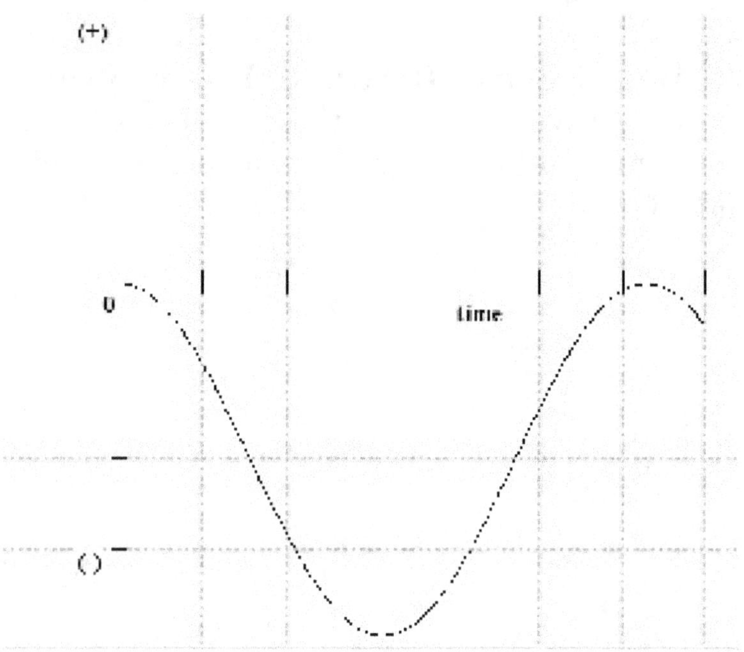

The impulse wave is emitted more as a short burst, or as a series of bursts, with the wave then going back to zero. By contrast, resident THOT/EMOT waves in the field emanate more continuous streams of energy.

Impulse waves are associated with quantum position (Herbert, 1985, p. 101), and stay fixated in place in the energy field. These are associated with intense emotions and fixated thoughts, often found in many forms of mental illness.

Resident waves are associated with the temporal sine wave family, where each sine wave represents a different value of energy. The energy value E is given by:

$E = hf$, where h is Planck's constant and f is the frequency of the wave.

Impulse waves powered by negative emotions have a fragmenting effect on the THOT/EMOT field, disrupting other THOT/EMOT waves. A mind dominated by negative emotions is therefore more chaotic, less focused and self-destructive. Impulse waves have a differentiative impact, segmenting $T/E(i)$s one from another.

In its most extreme form, this segmentation takes the form of dissociation, resulting in possible

fugue states, **derealization** and **dissociative identity disorder**.

THOT/EMOT waves predicated upon pure love generate huge energies. These waves have an integrative effect, combining other T/E components into its larger form.

These temporal sine waves have an integrative effect upon other waves, and tend to manifest longer lasting forms in the physical world.

AXIOM 3. Each static _kap(i)_ is an orbiting fixation, a satellite around the nucleus of the THOT/EMOT field. Each static _kap(i)_ has a resonant frequency (_f_) and a specific energy (_E_) expressed by:

Dalrymple's Law (1978):

$$E = \frac{mf^2}{SR\left(1 - \dfrac{f^2}{c^2}\right)}$$

m = mass of T/E fixation; *SR* is the square root; c is the speed of light.**

This means that as f increases and approaches c, the denominator of the equation approaches zero. Here, the energy (E) approaches infinity (Dalrymple, 1978).

A mind with a high frequency f is more enlightened, flexible, creative and expansive. If f approaches zero, then E also approaches zero. Here, a low f correlates with a dull, uncreative or intensely fixated mind.

LEMMA 1. The overall energy of the static satellite THOT-EMOT field is therefore given by:

$$E(total) = \sum_{i=1}^{n} \frac{m_i f_i^2}{SR\left(1 - \dfrac{f_i^2}{c^2}\right)}$$

LEMMA 2. Dynamic *kap(i)* components manifest waveforms continuously as the mind creates images, symbols and abstract products, powered by varying emotions at varying intensities.

These modify the overall energy field continuously, with the static field generating various bandwidths of specific frequencies, and the dynamic components playing over them like a *melody over rhythm.*

LEMMA 3. Phase-locking can occur, where many of the *kap(i)* may resonate at the same frequency, thereby generating a more powerful THOT/ EMOT wave and producing more immediate and powerful manifestations.

LEMMA 4. The structure of specific resident waveforms manifest in specific attributes within the individual's mind, emotions and behavior.

This parallels the association of attributes with waveforms found in general quantum theory (Herbert, 1985, p. 103). Since there exist a potentially infinite number of waveform families, the number of "*realities*" any individual can create are virtually infinite as well.

This point is well-exemplified by the vast diversity of personalities, as well as the inordinate states of psychosis and various personality disorders.

LEMMA 5. The spin attribute of the field is associated with the spherical harmonic family of waveforms (Herbert, 1985, p. 101), where each spherical harmonic gives a different value of spin magnitude and spin orientation.

The regions of vibration about the sphere are partitioned by a certain number n of nodal circles, a number m of which pass through the poles of the sphere.

The spin magnitude S is given by the total number of nodes n according to the rule:

$$S = hn,$$ where h is Planck's constant.

The more nodes m that go through the poles, the more the spin points in the polar direction z. For a given **spherical harmonic**, the spin orientation value $S(z)$ in the polar direction is given by:

$$S(z) = \frac{m^2}{n^2 + n},$$

(Herbert, 1985, p. 101).
For a given family of waveforms, the spin magnitude and orientation can take only certain discrete values, and thus are "*quantized*" and digitized.

AXIOM 4. Each THOT/EMOT component is a transverse wave, with THOT vs. EMOT aspects being perpendicular to one another, similar to electromagnetic waves.

Fluctuations in mood can color many waves of thought, just as specific thoughts can evoke specific waves of emotion.

Thoughts and emotions often occur together, although some thoughts may appear to be emotionless, and some feeling states may appear to evoke few cognitive correlates.

This formulation leads to a parallel to **Faraday's equation**...

AXIOM 5. *GRADIENT OF THOT (T)* = $\dfrac{d(EMOT)}{dt}$, **a change in thought (parallel to electricity) is a function of the derivative of emotional change (parallel to magnetism), over the derivative of time (t). In abbreviated form, this is:**

$$dT = \frac{dE}{dt}$$

A large emotional fluctuation can induce precipitant changes in thought flux. Rapid emotional shifts, as observed in borderline personality disorders, for example, coalesce with vast fluctuations in thought content.

Similarly...

LEMMA 1. GRADIENT OF EMOT = $\dfrac{d(THOT)}{dt}$ **, a change in emotion is a function of the derivative of thought flux, over the derivative of time.**

LEMMA 2. PARTIAL DERIVATIVES:
Different T/E components interact and influence each other, defined by partial derivatives. Suppose a given thought-form, T, is influenced by two emotional components, E(1) and E(2).

Then,
$$dT = \frac{\partial T}{\partial E(1)} dE(1) + \frac{\partial T}{\partial E(2)} dE(2)$$

This means that if the influence of E(1) is nonsignificant, this term drops out of the equation, and we are left with the fluctuation in T being defined by the derivative, or rate of change of T with respect to E(2), and vice versa if E(2) is non-significant.

In most situations, however, the rate of change of T will be defined by the combinatorics of partial derivatives as given in the equation.

This model can then be applied to any number of E(i) influences on T.

Similarly,
$$dE = \frac{\partial E}{\partial T(1)} dT(1) + \frac{\partial E}{\partial T(2)} dT(2)$$

Here, the fluctuation in an emotional component is a derivative of two or more thought components.

This model can be extended to any number of THOT or EMOT components.

LEMMA 3. PSYCHOLOGICAL DEFENSE mechanisms are described by partial derivatives. The act of repression modifies a situation where various cognitive and emotional aspects of the scenario are blocked from conscious awareness, and the resulting stored memory is a partial form of the original.

Suppose an individual who engages in repression encounters a situation influenced by the emotions of anger (E1), fear (E2), shame (E3) and guilt (E4). Suppose the person represses all of the emotions involved, except anger.

The modification of the THOT/EMOT field is described by:

$$dT = \frac{\partial T}{\partial E(1)}dE(1) + \frac{\partial T}{\partial E(2)}dE(2) + \frac{\partial T}{\partial E(3)}dE(3) + \frac{\partial T}{\partial E(4)}dE(4)$$

Here, the terms pertaining to E(2), E(3) and E(4) are cancelled out, leaving the thought modified on the conscious level by E(1) only, the anger.

The stored THOT/EMOT form is therefore:

$$dT = \frac{\partial T}{\partial E(1)} dE(1)$$

Note that the repressed components are stored unconsciously as resident waveforms, influencing the person's life until they are confronted, resolved and released.

LEMMA 4. Repressed T/E fixations cause the energy field to be unbalanced and lop-sided. This may induce the individual to attempt to compensate for the imbalance by creating counterbalancing T/E formations, in the form of further psychological defenses or other delusions (false beliefs).

Here, $w = (kap(1) + ... + kap(n)) + ... + (kap(1') + ... + kap(n'))$; each psychological defense mechanism *kap(i')* is created to counterbalance the repressed T/E component described by *kap(i)*.

Numerous *kap(i')*s may be created for each *kap(i)*, causing the energy field to become increasingly more occluded in its ability to transmute energy from the superconscious mind to the conscious mind.

LEMMA 5. CLUSTERING may occur, where T/E fixations congeal in specific areas of the field.

Masses of consciousness may form, where subfields of energy congeal and function as an independent entity within the general field.

LEMMA 6. MOOD DISORDERS are expressed as Fourier wave forms as follows:

UNIPOLAR/MAJOR DEPRESSION: The patient's static THOT-EMOT fixations tend to resonant with negative feelings and thoughts, such as self-defeat, worry, anxiety, self-deprecation, hopelessness and helplessness.

The amplitude of the wave can be great, and the duration of time that the patient remains in the major depression may be weeks, months or longer.

THOT-EMOT

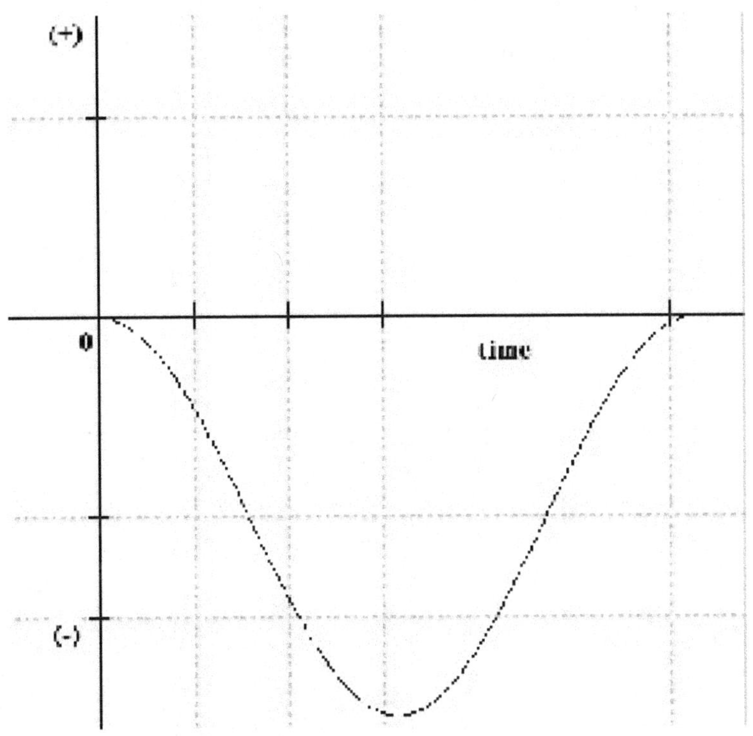

DYSTHYMIA: The patient's static THOT-EMOT waves show less amplitude than evidenced in major depression, with a shorter periodicity of depressive content.

THOT-EMOT

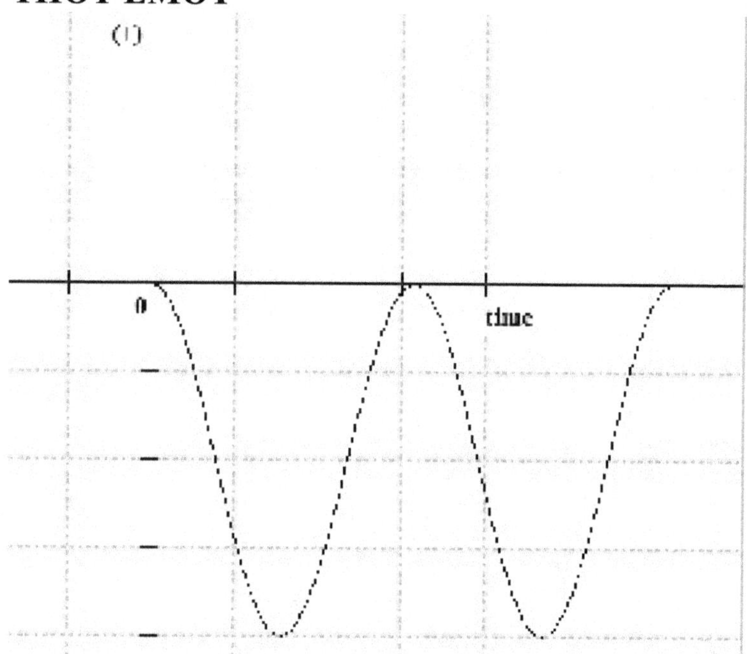

BIPOLAR DISORDER: The patient's static **THOT-EMOT** waves swing into the manic area for a period of time, with high amplitude and varying periodicity, followed by swings into the depressive area of significant amplitude and duration.

THOT-EMOT

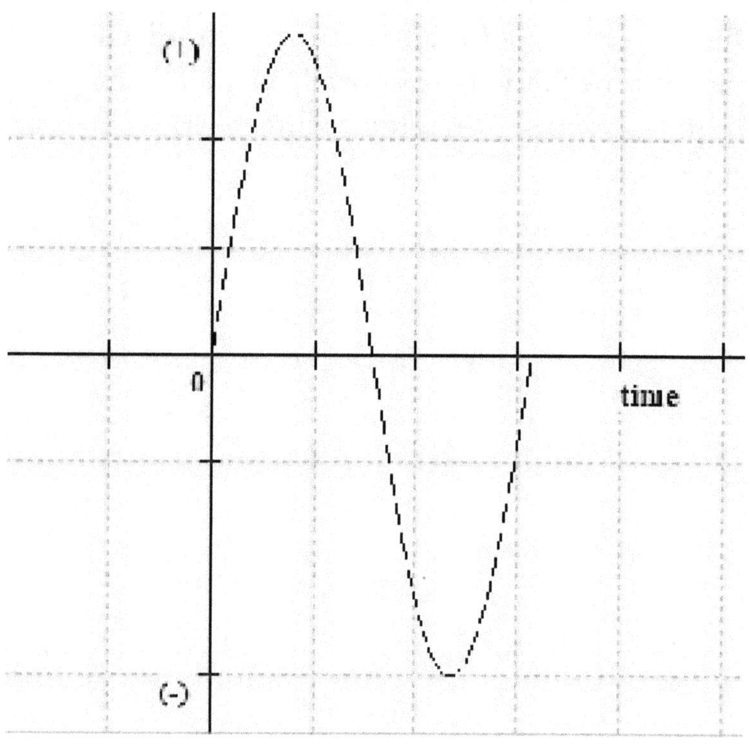

TYPE II BIPOLAR: The patient's static THOT-EMOT waves have a lesser amplitude during the manic component, but a depressive component equal to unipolar depression.

THOT-EMOT

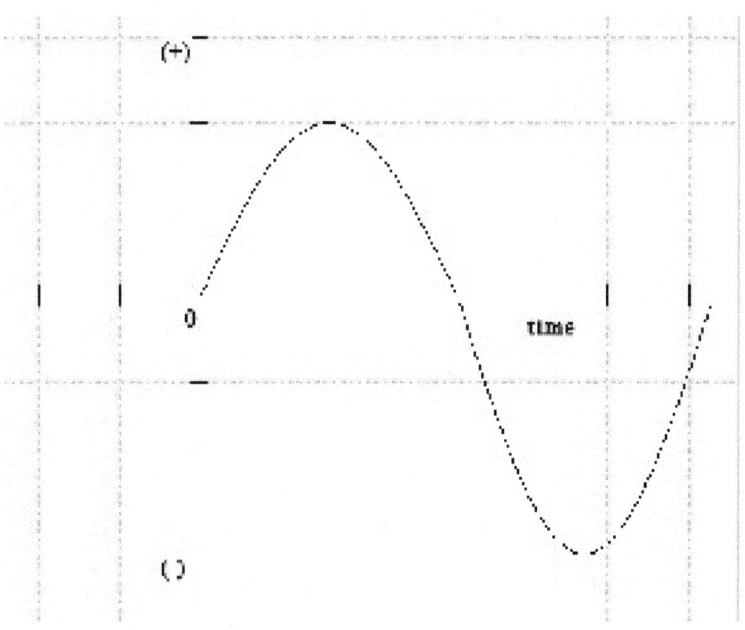

CYCLOTHYMIA: The patient's static THOT-EMOT waves are a lesser form of bipolar disorder, with lesser amplitude and shorter duration.

THOT-EMOT

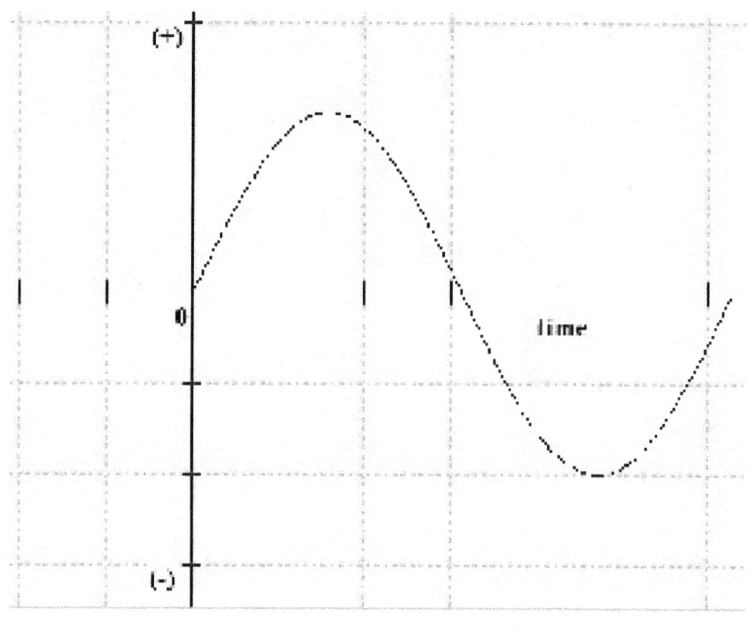

BORDERLINE PERSONALITY DISORDER:
The patient's static THOT-EMOT waves are highly erratic, with rapid mood swings, distorted thoughts and possible micropsychotic episodes. The amplitudes and durations of swings can vary widely.

THOT-EMOT

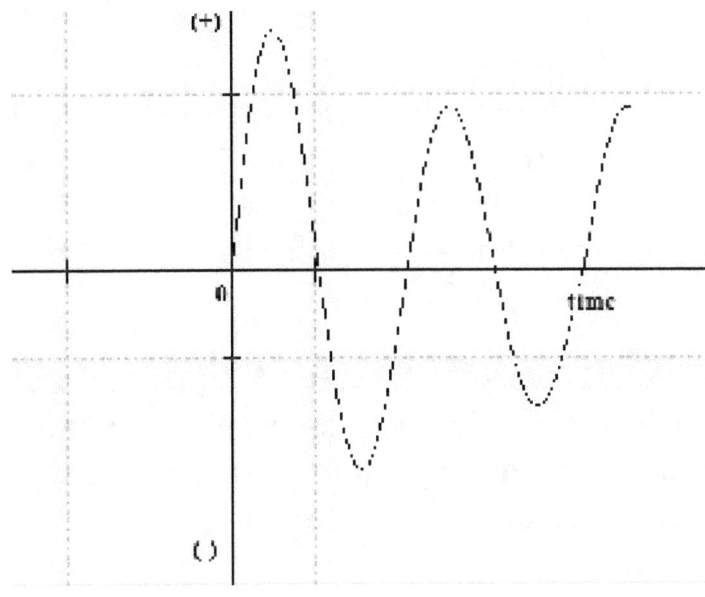

AXIOM 6. THOTON PARTICLE. THOT/ EMOT energy templates are foundations for material forms. **THOT/EMOT** emanations travel through space as waveforms, and interact with matter as particle forms.

The fundamental **THOT/EMOT** component is the **THOTON PARTICLE,** parallel to the photon for light and the graviton for gravity waves.

LEMMA 1. Static **THOT/EMOT** fixations and dynamic **THOT/EMOT** oscillations emanate continuous fields of energy, which over time tend to precipitate material forms by attracting and repelling specific particles of matter.

LEMMA 2. SYNCHRONICITY is produced in the life of the individual, as the **THOT/EMOT** currents attract people and events symbolic of the projected energy templates.

LEMMA 3. Each THOT/EMOT fixation manifests as both a waveform and a satellite within the energy field.

Each T/E has the static attributes of mass (M), charge (Q), and spin magnitude (S). Unlike elementary particles, T/E fixations can be transformed from static to dynamic state by the individual, who has the power to modify the mass, charge and spin magnitude.

They are therefore static only as long as they remain unmodified, which can be due to their presence in the unconscious mind, or are simply habits to which the individual pays no attention.

Dynamic attributes of each T/E fixation are positioned in the energy field, momentum, spin orientation and projective power.

Dynamic *kap(i)* elements can be transformed into a static state by habituation through learning, or through repression, where they are relegated to the unconscious domain.

Spin is given in one direction if the T/E formation is positive in nature, and in the opposite direction if negative in nature. Positive formations are attractive toward other elements, and negative formations are repulsive.

Positive waveforms combine in a sinusoidal manner, following the precepts of the Fourier pattern. Continuous negative waveforms may appear as more abrupt impulse waves or spindle waves, which tend to disintegrate or interfere with positive waves.

Projective power of each T/E fixation is the composite of waveforms emanating from the energy field, in a form focused by the T/E fixation. The T/E fixation acts like a lens, where energy arising from the nucleus of the field is modified by each **kap(i)** component of the overall waveform, w.

The long-term, deep level presence of T/E fixations can be overcome by a concentration of the will, by focusing the attention on specific visual imagery, especially when powered by consistently intense emotions.

The spin orientation of any given element can be changed, in order to eliminate the negative formations. Either short-term or long-term changes can be induced in the energy field.

Manifestations of the field occur continuously, whether the individual realizes it or not. Conscious control of this process can be attained by realization of how this process works, and by experimenting with it for verification and replication.

It is recommended that individuals only experiment with positive goals, emotions and actions, due to the reverberations that return to the source in like form.

This brings us to the next lemma.

LEMMA 4. For every THOT/EMOT emanation there is an equal and opposite reaction, which may occur as a returning waveform to its source, and/or as a material form manifestation.

This parallels Newton's third law, a well-established axiom in the physical universe (Dalrymple, 1989).

LEMMA 5. As THOT/EMOT emotionalized images occur in the conscious field, either from sensory input, perception, memory or imagination, the longer it is held in focus, the more energy will accrue to the emanation.

If the individual dwells upon any given T/E form, it becomes more likely to manifest in the individual's life, either directly or through synchronicity. If a T/E form has an especially strong desire or fear attached to it, it is empowered by the emotion to produce a more profound and immediate effect.

Individuals must beware what they desire or fear, for they are likely to experience it (Dalrymple, 1989).

To uncreate an undesired T/E form, the emotional component attached to it must be reduced to zero, and the thought released, forgiven, expiated. It is best to then replace it with a counter-thought comprised of a form and emotional component beneficial to the individual.

The probability of occurrence of any waveform is its intensity, I, which is equal to the square of the amplitude, A.

$$\text{Probability}(w) = I(w) = A^2.$$

Given a field with many waveforms resident within, the forms with the greatest intensity are therefore most likely to manifest in the individual's life in actual material form, or in terms of attracting or repelling events and other people who synchronize with the forms.

LEMMA 6. Parallels to Newtonian physics are found with the magnetic mass of emotional energy expressed by m, and the acceleration of thought waves by a, giving:

$F = ma$ **, the force of THOT/EMOT waves being mass times acceleration.**

LEMMA 7. Similarly, the momentum of THOT/ EMOT waves are given by:

$M = mv$**, momentum being the product of the magnetic mass of emotion times the velocity of thought.**

LEMMA 8. The EGO is a mass of magnetized/ emotionalized energy, where self-referent concepts, repressed emotions and defense mechanisms are held in place by delusional thoughts and petty beliefs.

The attractive force between two egos is given by:

$$F = \frac{M(1) \bullet M(2) \bullet G}{d^2}$$

where $M(i)$ is the mass of each ego, G is the egotistical constant, and d is the psychological distance between the two egos.

AXIOM 7. ENERGY FIELDS. The structure of the energy field is a series of concentric shells, with each shell ordained by a specific THOT/ EMOT fixation or a set of fixations.

LEMMA 1. THOT/EMOT shells form around the nucleus of the mind like electron shells around an atom, with the number and complexity of shells determining the nature of the personality.

The structure of these shells underlies covalent bonds and other interpersonal combinatorics (see Axiom 9).

LEMMA 2. The nucleus of the energy field is the SUPERCONSCIOUS MIND, composed of purely positive energy and receptive to and interactive with a vast array of energy frequencies.

LEMMA 3. CHAKRAS. Energy is transmuted from the superconscious level to the conscious level by the 7 power plant chakras of the endocrine system (Prophet and Spadaro, 2000), which act as transformers to increase or decrease the frequency of energy.

These are:

Base chakra: Adrenals.

The energy generated from this chakra is expressed by:

$$E(1) = hf(1)$$, where E is energy, h is Planck's constant, and $f(1)$ is the frequency of energy being transmitted through the chakra.

Soul chakra: Genitals and organs of elimination.

Here, $E(2) = hf(2)$.

Solar plexus chakra: Digestion, liver and pancreas.

$$E(3) = hf(3).$$

Heart chakra: Heart, thymus, circulatory system.

$$E(4) = hf(4).$$

Throat chakra: Thyroid, lungs, respiratory system.

$$E(5) = hf(5).$$

Third-eye chakra: Pituitary gland.

$$E(6) = hf(6).$$

Crown chakra: Pineal gland, cerebral cortex, nervous system.

$$E(7) = hf(7)$$.

Combining all the chakras gives:

$$E(total) = h((f(1) + f(2) + f(3) + f(4) + f(5) + f(6) + f(7))$$
, or:
$$E(total) = h\int f(i)$$.

Balancing each of the energy centers into a harmonic whole produces energy waves that manifest beautific results. If the centers are not harmonic, energy waves are projected of a discordant nature.

These are parallel to the keys of a musical scale. Certain keys combine to produce either chords or discordant noise. Notes and chords are combined to produce melodies and rhythms, or chaos.

Pursuant to **Axiom 3, Lemma 5**, we know that the spherical harmonics of the field are underlain by the contributory THOT/EMOT fixations, which interact with chakra functions.

LEMMA 4. Surrounding the nucleus is the concentric interface of the SUBCONSCIOUS MIND, which is designed to store information sourced from the superconscious mind, in order to drive the system in a deductive manner.

The subconscious mind forms as an interface between the superconscious mind at the nucleus and the external world. It is intended to act deductively, parallel to internal software, influencing the conscious mind to follow courses of action directed by wisdom and insight, as imprinted upon it by the superconscious mind.

However, the conscious mind instills many other streams of software onto the subconscious mind, including false beliefs and distorted emotions learned from the external world. This produces the satellites of THOT/EMOT fixation.

See **LEMMA 13** for an explanation of topological mappings, that occur between the Conscious and Superconscious Minds, onto or into the Subconscious Mind.

LEMMA 5. CRYSTALLIZED personality traits are generated by resonant, more permanent THOT/EMOT shells stored in the subconscious mind.

LEMMA 6. FLUID personality traits are generated by more transitory THOT/EMOT formations, which occur in the conscious mind or the preconscious mind as a result of sensory input, perception, memory, imagination and other neural synchronies.

LEMMA 7. The PRECONSCIOUS MIND is composed of THOT/EMOT forms, symbols, images and information immediately available to conscious awareness. These resonate between the subconscious and conscious levels.

LEMMA 8. Bands of concentric shells may occur, where specific **THOT/EMOT** foci resonate close to one another.

These bands are similar in THOT/EMOT frequency, forming a **FAMILY OF FREQUENCIES** (see Axiom 1, Lemma 3).

LEMMA 9. THOT/EMOT formations near the Superconscious nucleus reflect positive emotional fixations, and those near the subconscious or beyond may reflect positive or negative ones.

Positive fixations are more likely to underlie long-term couplings with other individuals, than are negative ones. Positive fixations create integrations of energy fields, and negative ones create disintegrations.

LEMMA 10. COGNITIVE SCHEMA. Positive emotions link together many positive thoughts, just as negative emotions key into many negative thoughts. Conversely, positive thoughts evoke positive emotions, and negative thoughts evoke negative emotions.

These THOT/EMOT connections comprise various cognitive schema, such that an entire lattice-work of connections can be brought into conscious awareness by a single thought or emotion.

LEMMA 11. Concentric shells may act as capacitors, where the emotional/magnetic charge of two respective shells may induce a reduction or enhancement of thought/electric flux between them.

Intensely fixated capacitor effects underlie **DISSOCIATIVE DISORDERS,** where different aspects of the THOT/EMOT field fragment and differentiate into separate fields.

Re-integrating the disparate fields is therefore the key to resolving **DISSOCIATIVE IDENTITY DISORDER, FUGUE STATES** and **POST TRAUMATIC STRESS DISORDER.**

Further disintegration of connectivity between THOT/EMOT forms can result in schizophrenia-like states of consciousness.

LEMMA 12. The development and functioning of the concentric shells is described by a MATHEMATICS OF MENTAL SPACE.

Using a polar coordinate system allows description of the field with a high energy nucleus of high frequency and positive polarity. The frequency decreases as the concentric THOT/EMOT shells move away from the nucleus, with more negative polarities occurring in the periphery of the field.

The vector of the polar coordinate system describes the attentional focus of consciousness, with the vector continuously moving as a function of free will, sensory input, memory and perceptual processes.

The concentric shells are held in position by the magnetic field of emotional energy, with electric currents of thought flowing around the surface of the shells. Each fluctuation in the emotional field induces changes in the flow of thought, and thought flow generates emotional field flux.

LEMMA 13. TOPOLOGY: Specific foci in the mind are projected from shell to shell, where elements of one shell may map surjectively, or onto another shell, or elements may map injectively, or into, another shell.

Mathematically, these mappings are described by:

Let S, S' be sets, and $F : S \rightarrow S'$ a mapping (Lang, 1966).

F is **INJECTIVE** if whenever t, u are elements of S, and t is not $= u$, then $F(t)$ is not $= F(u)$. Here, F maps S **INTO** S'.

This means that each element projected from one shell maps to a unique element in the second shell, but not all the points of the second shell are mapped to.

F is **SURJECTIVE** if the image of F is all of S', such that for any element w in S', there exists an element v in S such that $F(v) = w$. Here, F maps S **ONTO** S', such that all points of S are mapped.

LEMMA 14. These TOPOLOGICAL mappings describe various aspects of human communication, where one person (S) may think and see far beyond another (S'). Further, an element in a shell in S may map to an element in a completely different shell in S', or vice versa.

Specific mappings between people might be injective, but not surjective, or surjective, but not injective.

The defense mechanism of projection works in a surjective manner, where the individual projects his or her misperceptions onto another, regardless of what actually exists inside the other.

LEMMA 15. ISOMORPHISMS:

Let $F: V \rightarrow W$ be a linear map, assume F is injective and surjective. Then F is invertible and an ISOMORPHISM.

This would occur if two fields mapped back and forth, point for point, perfectly. This would constitute perfect communication.

LEMMA 16. METAMORPHISMS. Most human communication can only come as close as metamorphisms, where much is mapped, but not point for point.

Here, much communication is lost between people, due to translation problems, differential knowledge and experiential biases, misperceptions, cultural differences, subterfuge and a host of other issues.

AXIOM 8. Personality disorders (PD) illustrate different fixations of THOT/ EMOT waveforms.

The following discussion of personality disorders is derived from Millon (1981), with the mathematical applications predicated upon the precepts of quantum field psychology.

The mathematical analysis of these disorders and their relationships to the concentric shells of THOT/EMOT fixation are described below.

Briefly, these T/E shells and their emotionalized, magnetized valences take the form of:

INNER CORE OF BEING

SOFTWARE CREATED TO DRIVE

FIRST SHELL

SECOND SHELL

THIRD SHELL

SUPER SUB CONSCIOUS LEVELS	SELF (+) OR (-)	SELF TRUST OR DISTRUST ATTACH OR DISATTACH	OTHERS TRUST OR DISTRUST ATTACH OR DISATTACH	CONTROL SELF (+ , -) OTHERS (+ , -)

Here, the superconscious and conscious minds write onto the subconscious mind software, where various attitudes, beliefs and emotions are stored, which then drive the system deductively.

The self-concept learned from external world interactions is either positive or negative or both, in various combinations of thoughts and emotions.

One then attaches to the self, or detaches. More T/E shells form as concepts of others are created, with trust and attachment growing, or distrust and detachment.

A sense of self-control and control over one's environment then evolves, or not. Various defense mechanisms are created, composed of various T/E combinations, which then ward off incipient anxiety, fears and threats from consciousness, but which also block and distort energy, perception, creativity and bonding with others.

Mathematically, we can express the first level as being that of self vs. other, as X.

Let the next level be analogous to Freud's oral level, constituting trust vs. mistrust, expressed as X^2, a derivation of the first level, X.

Let the next level be X^3, analogous to Freud's anal level, or control vs. dyscontrol.

Let the next be X^4, parallel to the phallic level, or attachment to versus detachment from others, and the point of solidification of the ego.

The energy dynamics of the system can be expressed as:

$$E = aX + bX^2 + cX^3 + dX^4$$

The rate of change of energy, or the velocity of energy, is given by the derivative:

$$\frac{dE}{dt} = E' = 2bX + 3cX^2 + 4dX^3$$

This is the speed of thought and emotion, which is more of a constant speed when the thoughts and emotions are focused on specific and continuous foci.

As thoughts and emotions change, the rate of change of the velocity of the energy gives the acceleration of energy, or:

$$\frac{dE'}{dt} = E'' = 2b + 6cX + 12dX^2$$

Strong emotional outbursts or changes reflect accelerations or decelerations of thought and emotion.

Applying these concepts to the personality disorders, we have:

LEMMA 1. The ANXIETY CLUSTER of personality disorders represents individuals who frequently generate waveforms of fearfulness and repulsion toward specific individuals, objects or situations.

(1) **THE AVOIDANT PERSONALITY DISORDER** evidences extreme social inhibition, introversion, hypersensitivity to rejection but a strong desire for affection. They are often lonely and bored, with acute anxiety, low self-esteem and are intensely self-conscious.

They may see ridicule and rejection where none exists, and are terrified of the slightest risk of humiliation.

KEY COMPONENTS:

* LOW SELF-ESTEEM
* SELF-REJECTION
* DESIRE FOR BONDING
* FEAR OF BONDING DUE TO FEAR OF
    REJECTION

The **AVOIDANT PD** has a waveform characterized by:

$$w = kap(i) + kap(j) + kap(m) + kap(n)$$

where $kap(i)$ is (low self-esteem), $kap(j)$ is (desire for bonding), $kap(m)$ is (fear of bonding), and $kap(n)$ is (fear of rejection).

By desiring and fearing *social bonding* at the same time, the wave forms mask each other and can cancel each other out, with the individual caught in a continuous struggle.

The desire for bonding might motivate the person to try and reach out in a more precipitous manner, but fear is easily evoked due to low self-esteem, again inhibiting and frustrating the attempts.

These personalities are differentially diagnosed from SCHIZOID PDs, who do not care about criticism or attachment to others. The AVOIDANT PD may co-occur with DEPENDENT PD.

AVOIDANT PDs are differentiated from social phobia in that AVOIDANTS are often a worse case, being more generalized and more intense. However, both of these conditions may respond to the same treatments.

(2) **THE DEPENDENT PD** is the next member of the **ANXIETY CLUSTER.** The **DEPENDENT PD** has an intense need to be taken care of, and are highly manipulative in attaining these needs.

On the surface, they are submissive, panic at being alone and are poor in their selection of mates.

They have a low trust of self, coupled with a high trust of others.

They may bond with a **NARCISSISTIC PD** and cling to that person no matter what. Since the **NARCISSISTIC PD** likes being worshipped, this bond initially might seem to work.

However, each personality is unstable and this form of bonding usually proves to be superficial and may well disintegrate as the pressures and stressors of life ensue.

The **DEPENDENT PD** subordinates his or her needs to others, lacks confidence and has low self-esteem. They often feel helpless, despite being competent at work.

They need and seek constant reassurance for even minor decisions. They feel selfless, and often fail to express their individuality. They are often docile and self-effacing.

The disorder may be comorbid with other anxiety disorders, such as social phobia, panic disorder, generalized anxiety disorder and eating disorders.

The disorder overlaps with **BORDERLINE**, **HISTRIONIC** and **AVOIDANT PDs**.

KEY COMPONENTS:

* LOW TRUST OF SELF
* HIGH TRUST OF OTHERS
* HIGH NEED TO CONTROL OTHERS TO
  FEED THE SELF

This disorder is characterized by a waveform where:

(low self-esteem)	(low trust of self)	(childlike attachment)	(separation anxiety)	(highly controlling)
$w = kap(i) +$	$kap(j)$	$+kap(m)$	$+kap(n)$	$+kap(q)$

(3) **THE OBSESSIVE-COMPULSIVE PD** has low self-esteem, generalized anxieties, a lack of trust for others, a high need for order, and ritualized behaviors.

They express perfectionism and a supreme attention to detail, where they check and double check things constantly to avoid making any mistakes.

These patients may check the door on their house or apartment countless times before going out. They waste much time on trivial details, often not finishing projects. They indulge in a high degree of self-criticism.

They engage in deprivation, depriving themselves and others of comforts. They avoid leisure as a waste of time, and can never fully relax. They are conscientious, competent and devoted to work. They are often inflexible on moral and ethical issues, stingy and selfish with money.

They have trouble delegating work to others, since they do not trust others. They have difficulty in relationships, find it hard to express emotions and dislike dealing with the emotions of others.

The personality disorder is differentially diagnosed from the full-blown obsessive-compulsive disorder, who has intrusive obsessive thoughts that cause intense anxiety and can only be reduced by performing frequent rituals. Much time daily is thus wasted.

The **OBSESSIVE-COMPULSIVE PD** overlaps with **NARCISSISTIC, ANTISOCIAL** and **SCHIZOID PDs.**

KEY COMPONENTS:

* LOW SELF-ESTEEM
* GENERALIZED ANXIETIES
* FEAR OF INABILITY TO CONTROL
  THINGS
* RITUALIZED BEHAVIORS

$$w = \underset{\substack{\text{(low} \\ \text{self-} \\ \text{esteem)}}}{kap(i)} + \underset{\substack{\text{(general-} \\ \text{ized} \\ \text{anxieties)}}}{kap(j)} \ \text{“} \ \underset{\substack{\text{(fear of} \\ \text{inability} \\ \text{to} \\ \text{control)}}}{kap(k)} + \underset{\substack{\text{(ritual-} \\ \text{ized} \\ \text{behaviors)}}}{kap(n)}$$

(4) **THE PASSIVE-AGGRESSIVE PD** resists others in manipulative and deceitful ways, just for the sake of sabotaging others. They have problems with authority figures, and cycle between submissiveness and defiance.

They are grateful and compliant when praised, but can become enraged when not given their way or when criticized even slightly. They are envious of others, jealous, rumor-mongering and back-stabbing.

They block the desires and actions of others, while pretending to be innocent. They avoid responsibility, dumping all responsibility on others when possible.

They refuse to comply with dictates at work, despite appearing glib and personable on the surface.

KEY COMPONENTS:

* NARCISSISTIC SELF-LOVE
* ANGER AT OTHERS
* FEAR OF EXPRESSING ANGER AT OTHERS
* AVOIDANCE OF RESPONSIBILITY
* ACTING OUT EMOTIONS THROUGH SABOTAGING OTHERS

	fear of		sabo-tage
narcissistic self-love	expres-sing	avoid	others
anger at others	anger	responsi-bility	
$w =$		kap	kap
$kap(i) +$	$kap\ (j)$ (m)	$kap(n)+$	(q)

LEMMA 2. The BIZARRE CLUSTER of personality disorders express different forms of odd, eccentric, distrustful and suspicious behavior, often with social withdrawal or social inappropriateness.

(1.) **THE PARANOID PD** has a pervasive mistrust of others, is suspicious and tends to see oneself as blameless. They disown responsibility for what happens in relationships. They are constantly on guard for attacks from others, and often misinterpret situations where they blame others for their own negative, suspicious perceptions.

They project their own impulses onto others, blaming them for all manner of evil intentions. They doubt the words and actions of others in general, are hypersensitive, and read into situations threatening messages which are not there.

As they project their misperceptions onto others, they are performing various degrees of

SURJECTIVE mappings. They may indulge in **PROJECTIVE IDENTIFICATION**, where they project onto others and then react to the projections.

They refuse to forgive or forget, are vengeful and quick to anger. They can be dangerous, and are potentially assaultive or even homicidal. They may experience micropsychotic episodes, but most of the time are in reality contact - their reality.

They find it difficult to relax, are often busy with work, and dislike others being in their space. They are differentially diagnosed from paranoid schizophrenics, who exhibit greater loss of reality contact, with possible delusions, hallucinations, cognitive disorder and affective distortions.

KEY COMPONENTS:
* REJECTION SYNDROME, EASILY TRIGGERED
* INTENSE DISTRUST OF OTHERS
* PROJECTION OF OWN IMPULSES ONTO OTHERS

* OVERT HOSTILITY TOWARD OTHERS

	(in- tense	(projec- tion	(overt hostility
(rejecti on	dis- trust	of own impulses	
syn- drome)	of others)	onto others)	toward others)
$w =$ $kap(i)\ +$	kap $(j)\ +$	$kap(m)+$	$kap(n)$

(2) **THE SCHIZOID PD** appears cold and aloof to others, and withdrawn from social relationships. They often evidence anhedonia, seeking and taking little pleasure from activities in life, including sex.

They rarely experience strong emotions, positive or negative. They might be highly intelligent, but may find themselves embarrassed by social contacts, and are happiest alone.

They tend to lack a need for love, belonging or approval.

KEY COMPONENTS:

* LACK OF EMOTIONAL ATTACHMENT TO SELF, TO DESIRES OR FEARS

* LACK OF EMOTIONAL ATTACHMENT TO OTHERS OR TO GOALS IN LIFE

		(lack of	(lack
(lack of	(lack of	attach-	of
emotional	desires	ment	goals
connec-	or		
tion	fears)	to others)	in life)
to self)			

$$w = kap(i) + kap(j) + ... + kap(m) + kap(n)$$

(3) **THE SCHIZOTYPAL PD** evidences a high degree of introversion, interpersonal deficits, cognitive and perceptual distortions, and eccentricities in communication and behavior.

They exhibit bizarre thoughts, perceptions and speech. They maintain reality contact for the most part, but can have micropsychotic episodes, or longer transient psychotic episodes.

They may indulge in superstitious thinking, may believe they have magical powers and engage in magical rituals. They might exhibit ideas of reference, believing that words and gestures of others have special meaning toward them.

They might believe they are telepathic, have a special mission in life, are acutely self-conscious in public, often lost in fantasy and tangential thinking. They might miss the point often, but are not totally incoherent.

They generally have a peculiar thought structure and a loosening of ties to reality. They lack the ability to integrate their thoughts - or their life - together.

They show narcissistic thinking and suspicious beliefs, attentional deficits and difficulty concentrating.

The disorder may be part of a spectrum of schizophrenic disorders.

KEY COMPONENTS:

* INCOHERENT SENSE OF SELF
* INCOHERENT SENSE OF OTHERS
* DISTORTED EMOTIONS
* BIZARRE COGNITIONS AND BELIEFS
* INABILITY TO FORM STABLE
  RELATIONSHIPS OR BONDS

$$w = kap(i) + kap(j) + kap(k) + kap(m) + kap(n)$$

(fragmented sense of self) + (fragmented sense of others) + (distorted emotions) + (bizarre cognitions) + (poor bonds)

LEMMA 3. THE ACTING OUT CLUSTER are more dramatic, exhibiting erratic, highly labile moods. They tend to act out their emotional issues and their antisocial impulses, evoking involvement with legal and mental health systems.

THE HISTRIONIC PD loves to be the center of attention - or they might throw a temper tantrum to get it. They often act out for attention, are flamboyant, dramatic and have highly labile moods.

They often exhibit rapid mood swings if not getting the attention they seek, and may be seductive and indulge in sexual teasing. They might expose themselves to others to get a reaction.

They are often highly manipulative in relationships, may be dependent on others and constantly seek approval. Shallow, insincere and overly reactive, they often destroy relationships.

They may avoid details because it requires longer concentration.

KEY COMPONENTS:
* NARCISSISTIC SELF-IMAGE
* DISREGARD FOR RIGHTS OF OTHERS
* DEPENDENCY NEED FOR ATTENTION
* IMPULSIVE MOODS
* ACTING OUT OF EMOTIONS

(narcis-sistic self-image) (disre-gard rights of oth-ers) (depen-dency need for atten-tion) (imp-pul-sive moods) (act-ing out emo-tions)

$$w = kap(i) + kap(j) + kap(k) + kap(m) + kap(n)$$

(2) **THE NARCISSISTIC PD** has a high degree of self-importance, and loves to be admired, even worshipped. They have a lack of empathy for the rights, concerns, needs and feelings of others.

Being grandiose, they over-exaggerate their own accomplishments, and under-exaggerate the accomplishments of others. They often can't understand why others don't see things their way.

Bragging often, they seek the company of important others, and are amazed when they are rebuffed. They often take advantage of others, and feel they are empowered to do so.

Children are inherently narcissistic, and must acquire the insight that others have feelings and rights on an equal level. The **NARCISSISTIC PD** is often envious of others, and believes others are envious of them.

They can't stand criticism, which makes them feel humiliated and full of rage. The grandiosity is a cover for low self-esteem.

They are differentially diagnosed from the **HISTRIONIC PD**, who are more needy, promiscuous, want to be noticed and the center of attention. The **NARCISSISTIC PD** is more aloof, exploitative, wants to be admired by others, even worshipped. Both are exhibitionistic and often promiscuous.

The NARCISSISTIC PD resists therapy, because they are sure they are perfect already. They often feel superior to the therapist and are resistant to the long-term therapy needed.

KEY COMPONENTS:
* PROFOUND SELF-LOVE, AS A MASK FOR LOW SELF-ESTEEM
* DISREGARD FOR THE RIGHTS OF OTHERS
* EASILY HUMILIATED
* RAGE TOWARD OTHERS

	(pro-found self-love as a mask)	(disre-gard for rights of others	(easily humil-iated)	(rage at oth ers)
(low self-esteem)				

$$w = kap(i) + kap(j) + kap(m) + kap(n) + kap(q)$$

(3) THE ANTISOCIAL PD has no empathy for the rights, needs, property or well-being of others. They are often deceitful, manipulative, aggressive, irritable, impulsive and show no remorse for the damage they do to others.

These individuals are found in the ranks of con artists, criminals and politicians. They are often loners and aggressive toward others. They may openly repel others. Their exploitation of others is aimed at domination, prestige and imagined superiority.

KEY COMPONENTS:

* NARCISSISTIC SELF-LOVE
* DISRESPECT FOR OTHERS
* ANGER AT OTHERS
* ACTING OUT TO HARM OTHERS

$$w = \underset{\substack{\text{(narcis-}\\ \text{sistic}\\ \text{self-love)}}}{kap(i)} + \underset{\substack{\text{(disrespect}\\ \text{for the}\\ \text{rights}\\ \text{of others)}}}{kap(j)} + \underset{\substack{\text{(anger}\\ \text{at}\\ \text{others)}}}{kap(m)} + \underset{\substack{\text{(acting}\\ \text{out}\\ \text{to}\\ \text{harm}\\ \text{others)}}}{kap(n)}$$

(4) **THE BORDERLINE PD** exhibits huge mood swings, intense fear of rejection, are highly impulsive, moody and erratic. They act out impulses readily, are often promiscuous, may be involved in drug and alcohol use, and have unstable relationships.

A disorder of affective and cognitive disturbance, they have highly conditional self-esteem that covers a rejection syndrome. Their sense of rejection can be easily triggered, with the slightest glance, word or action by another.

They suffer from an identity problem, with an unstable sense of self. They feel love/hate toward themselves, and often intensely fear abandonment. When slighted, they may react with extreme outbursts, manipulations and abuse toward the imagined perpetrator.

They may swing from over-idealization of friends and lovers, followed by bitter disillusionment. They have a low tolerance for frustration, with feelings of emptiness.

They may indulge in self-destructive binges of gambling, drinking, promiscuity, self-mutilation, suicidality or binge-eating.

Self-mutilation may reduce their anxiety and dysphoria, and a significant number do eventually commit suicide. Others have periods of transient psychoses, hallucinations, paranoid beliefs, body image distortions, dissociative symptoms and delusions.

Parallel to the paranoid personality disorder, they may readily project their misperceptions onto others, performing various degrees of SURJECTIVE mappings. They may indulge in PROJECTIVE IDENTIFICATION, where they project onto others and then react to the projections.

The disorder co-occurs with HISTRIONIC, DEPENDENT, ANTISOCIAL and SCHIZOTYPAL PDs.

KEY COMPONENTS:

* LOVE / HATE OF SELF
* REJECTION SYNDROME
* LABILE MOODS
* COGNITIVE / AFFECTIVE DISTORTIONS
* POSSIBLE *MICROPSYCHOTIC* EPISODES

(love/ hate of self)	(rejecti on syn- drome)	(labile moods)	(cogni-tive/ affective distor-tions)

$$w = kap(i) + kap(j) + kap(m) + kap(n)$$

AXIOM 9. Human relationships are energy couplings produced between two or more people, forming lattice-like energy bonds between them, composed of integrations of attractive and repulsive forces.

THOT/EMOT components map back and forth between the individuals, *injectively* and or *surjectively*, connecting them at multiple points of thought and feeling.

Entire spider-like webs surround people in relationships as they are pushed and pulled by these forces.

LEMMA 1. The characteristic THOT-EMOT waves between individuals are given by:

person 1   person 2

$$\sum_{k=1}^{2} w(k) = \sum_{p=1}^{n} kap(1,p) + \sum_{q=1}^{m} kap(2,q)$$

where k = spatial frequency, a = amplitude, p = phase. Each *kap(1, i)* or *kap(2, j)* can be a static or dynamic THOT/EMOT formation. More complex human relationships are described by expanding integrals, since Fourier waves are additive.

The Fourier waves can interact in a manner that causes one wave to mask or cancel another, in a subtractive influence. Other waves may interact to enhance each other by increasing their amplitudes. Still others may interact where one entrains, or drives the other.

When personality disorders connect, one wave compensates for another, but creates an unstable coupling.

LEMMA 2. The SUPERPOSITION PRINCIPLE describes how waveforms meet and interact, with amplitudes combining to a limit, beyond which non-linearity may occur, if amplitudes become too large.

A simplicity therefore exists between wave interactions, allowing a description of group interactions which manifest as a function of integrating the contributory sources (Herbert, 1985, p. 73).

LEMMA 3. COVALENT BONDS. Energy couplings between individuals can take the form of covalent bonds, where the superfluidity of THOT/EMOT formations of one individual may become attached to the deficit field of another.

Some of the possible combinations are **OBSESSIVE-COMPULSIVE PD** with **HISTRIONIC PD**, and **NARCISSISTIC PD** with **DEPENDENT PD**.

For example, the superfluous need for order expressed by the **OCD** patient initially helps to bring order to the **HISTRIONIC**, and the emotional expressivity of the **HISTRIONIC** provides a vicarious outlet for the **OCD**.

However, these connections are superficial, and the underlying instability of the fields in many cases ordains a short-term coupling.

LEMMA 4. MALE-FEMALE bonds, if harmonious, have the potential for generating enormous amounts of synergy, where the opposite poles of energy expressed by female and male (parallel to magnetic poles) induce expanding streams of thought energy exchange (parallel to electrical current).

When the male and female are not in harmony, vast perturbations of chaos and discord may result.

AXIOM 10. Consciousness is an expanding or contracting tensor energy field which interacts with and interrelates to the entire universe, which is also a tensor field.

Every particle and wave of energy interacts with every other particle and wave of energy on a continuous basis. The individual controls the rate of expansion or contraction of the field by his or her thoughts and emotions and will power.

LEMMA 1. Personality disorders constrict or distort the energy field as a function of the person's delusions (false beliefs) and unbalanced emotions.

LEMMA 2. Each THOT/EMOT fixation generates a SUBSPACE of the energy field of mind.

Each SUBSPACE, z, is of a larger space, v, defined as:

$z = v - n$, where n = any number less than v.

LEMMA 3. Each combination of THOT/EMOT fixations creates a DIMENSION of mind.

Each DIMENSION is defined as:

$w(i,...,k) = kap(i) + ... + kap(k)$

As the dimensions of one's perceptions approaches infinity:

$w(i,.......,k) \rightarrow v$, where v = the total space of the universe.

LEMMA 4. THOT/EMOT cycles, or *w*-waves, composed of multiple *kap(i)*, can be phase-locked to super-positive thoughts, seeing the good in all things at all times, projecting love to all other beings at all times, producing an infinite magnitude of being that is transcendent of this world.

Amplitudes of THOT/EMOT waves approach infinity if one phase-locks all waves into increasing amplitudes. Here,

$$E \rightarrow \infty.$$

If an individual entrains all of his or her thoughts and emotions with super-positive foci of love for all, and hope and joy, then that person's life becomes more successful, resilient and transcendent of the illusions of the world.

The word *heaven,* in Greek, means expansion.

LEMMA 5.   QUANTUM FIELDS. As one resolves each THOT/EMOT fixation in the satellite field, the connection between the superconscious mind at the nucleus and the conscious mind is increased by quantum leaps.

Each T/E fixation is a filter, blocking and distorting conscious access to superconscious insights and realizations. Removing each filter allows the breadth and depth of consciousness to expand, enhancing the quantum field.

Freud's work on catharsis is an earlier expression of this concept.

LEMMA 6. SUPERCONSCIOUSNESS. When all THOT/EMOT fixations are resolved, the superconscious mind at the nucleus is allowed to project fully to all levels of the conscious mind in peripheral levels.

This produces an ISOMORPHISM between the superconscious mind and all other levels of the mind, an expansion of consciousness ordained by the dimensions integrated.

Illuminated individuals throughout history, those who have become spiritual prophets, are those who have resolved all of their negative THOT/EMOT fixations and attained *God-Consciousness*.

LEMMA 7. As each THOT/EMOT fixation is resolved and its energy impedance removed, it allows the individual to bond with more individuals. This acts as a catalyst to release increasing cycles of energy flow between the individuals.

As more and more people connect with love, the balance of creative power on the planet shifts from the manifestation of negative external conditions to much more positive ones.

LEMMA 8. MANIFESTATION. As the energy of the mind approaches higher and higher levels, the ability to materially manifest the nature of one's THOT/EMOT foci increases.

Recalling Axiom 3:

$$E = \frac{mf^2}{SR\left(1 - \dfrac{f^2}{c^2}\right)}$$

where m = mass of T/E fixations; SR is the square root; c is the speed of light.

As f approaches c, the denominator of the equation approaches zero and the energy (E) approaches infinity (Dalrymple, 1978).

AXIOM 11. PLANETARY CONSCIOUSNESS.
THOT/EMOT templates held in the minds of billions of people worldwide interact with the entire planet, influencing all other living creatures on earth, the geomagnetic field, the weather, tidal variations and earthquakes.

LEMMA 1. When minds are trained to think negative thoughts, experience negative emotions and expect negative things to happen, the resulting chaos experienced in the world is profound.

Witness the world today, misguided, misdirected, misinformed.

LEMMA 2. When minds are trained to think positive thoughts, experience positive emotions and expect positive things to happen, the resulting beautiful things experienced in the world are even more profound.

LEMMA 3. The evolution of forms documented by Darwin (1859) is a subset of the evolution of consciousness, with forms providing vehicles for the manifestation of consciousness.

Darwin's seminal work in documenting changes in form missed the deeper issue of true function - to provide vehicles for evolving levels of consciousness.

Darwin's inability to explain rapid changes in form documented in sedimentation levels is a reflection of his restricted paradigm of adaptation.

A more feasible explanation may be found in DNA shifts occurring, as postulated by Gariaev and Poponin (2002).

AXIOM 12. TRAINING. Human beings throughout the world can be trained to harmonize and focus their thoughts and emotions in order to produce in their lives massive success, happiness and prosperity.

Much research exists in the area of psychoneuroimmunology and other areas to evidence the profound influence of the mind and emotions on the body, either for success, health and happiness, or for failure, disease and death.

Training systems need to be advanced worldwide to promote these ends.

LEMMA 1. GLOBAL TRAINING. Training the entire planet in these principles is a possible advent to world peace and the end of all manufactured wars, depressions, inflations, hunger and tyranny.

Societal pathologies and parasitologies feed on entraining human thoughts and emotions on negative imagery, symbols and fears, which enslave the mind and derange the society.

CONCLUSIONS

The development, structure and functions of the human mind can be described by mathematical principles and the laws of physics, constituting the basic precepts of quantum field psychology.

The principles described in this book are embryonic and are intended to inspire more research in this field, with the goal being to merge physical with psychological sciences.

The formulation and description of psychological processes in terms of physics and mathematics may facilitate greater predictivity in human behavior, as well as new therapeutic avenues of intervention in human pathology and human potential.

Future research is needed to: (a) broaden and refine mathematical models of thought and emotion predicated upon quantum physics; (b) investigate the impact of thought and emotion on DNA, RNA, cellular functions, and the overall bioenergy field; (c) investigate mind-to-mind communication, and human mind to animal and plant functions; (d) investigate the expansion of consciousness to more transcendent levels.

REFERENCES

Adam, N., Rosner, B.S., Hosick, E.C., & Clark, D.L. (1971). Effect of anesthetic drugs on time production and alpha rhythm. *Perception & Psychophysics*, 10, 133-136. In Coren, S., Ward, L.,& Enns, J. *Sensation and perception.* 6th Ed. New York: John Wiley & Sons.

Backster, C. (1968). "Evidence of a primary Perception in Plant Life," *International Journal of Parapsychology*, Vol. 10, No. 4.

Baddeley, A.D. (1966). Time estimation at reduced body temperature. *American Journal of Psychology*, 79, 475-479. In Coren, S., Ward, L.,& Enns, J. *Sensation and perception.* 6th Ed. New York: John Wiley & Sons.

Bandler, R., &, LaValle,J. (1996). *Persuasion engineering.* Capitola, CA: Meta Publications, Inc.

Capra, F. (2000). *The tao of physics.* 4th Ed. Boston: Shamballa Publications, Inc

Carlson, N. (1981). *Physiology of behavior*. 2nd Ed. Boston: Allyn and Bacon, Inc.

Cohen, L.W., & Ehrlich, G. (1963). *The structure of the real number system*. Princeton, NJ: D. Van Nostrand Company, Inc.

Coren, S., Ward, L.,& Enns, J. (2004). *Sensation and perception*. 6th Ed. New York: John Wiley & Sons.

Dalrymple, R. (1978). *Keys to genius*. Estes Park, CO: Celestial Gifts Publishing.

Dalrymple, R. (1985). *Increase your power of creative thinking in eight days*. Chester, MD: Celestial Gifts Publishing.

Dalrymple, R. (1989). *The inner manager*. Chester, MD: Celestial Gifts Publishing.

Dalrymple, R. (2004). *Quantum field psychology*. First Edition. N. Ft. Myers, FL: Celestial Gifts Publishing.

Dalrymple, R. (2016). *8 Days to creative power*. N. Ft. Myers, FL: Celestial Gifts Publishing.

Dalrymple, R. (2017). *I love you God.* N. Ft. Myers, FL: Celestial Gifts Publishing.

Dalrymple, R. (2019). *Principia mathematica psychica: Mathematical principles of the mind.* In production. Ft. Myers, FL: Celestial Gifts Publishing.

Darwin, C. (1998). *Origin of species*. New York: The Modern Library.

Emoto, M. (2004). *The hidden message in water*. Hillsboro, OR: Beyond Words Publishing, Inc.

Flanagan, G.P. (1997). *Pyramid power*. Anchorage, AK: Earthpulse Press.

Frankenhauser, M. (1959). *The estimation of time.* Stockholm: Almqvist & Wiksell. In Coren, S., Ward, L.,& Enns, J. *Sensation and perception.* 6th Ed. New York: John Wiley & Sons.

Gariaev, P. & Poponin, V. (2002). The DNA phantom effect: Direct measurement of a new field in the vacuum substructure. URL: http://twm.co.nz/DNAPhantom.htm.

Guillen, M. (1995). *Five equations that changed the world.* New York: MJF Books.

Harris. C. (2003). *NLP made easy.* London: Harper Collins.

Herbert, N. (1985). *Quantum reality: Beyond the new physics.* New York: Anchor Books.

Hixson, J. "Twins prove 'electronic' ESP," *New York Herald Tribune,* Oct. 25, 1965, *Science,* Oct. 15, 1965. In Ostander, S., & Schroeder, L. *Psychic discoveries behind the iron curtain.* NJ: Prentice-Hall.

Hoagland, H. (1933). The physiological control of judgement of duration: Evidence for a chemical clock. *Journal of General Psychology, 9*, 267-287. In Coren, S., Ward, L.,& Enns, J. *Sensation and perception.* 6th Ed. New York: John Wiley & Sons.

Hummel, J. (1967). *Introduction to vector functions.* Reading, MA: Addison- Wesley Publishing Company.

James, W. (1890). *The principles of psychology.* New York: Holt.

Jung, C. (1963). *Memories, dreams, reflections.* Rev. Ed. Ed. A. Jaffe. Trans. Richard and Clara Winston. New York: Vintage Books.

Kirk, R. (1968). *Experimental design: Procedures for the behavioral sciences.* Belmont, CA: Brooks/ Cole Publishing Company.

Kuhn, T.S. (1966). *The structure of scientific revolutions.* 3rd Ed. Chicago, IL: The University of Chicago Press.

Lang, S. (1966). *Linear algebra.* New York: Addison-Wesley.

Larson, H. (1969). *Introduction to probability theory and statistical inference.* New York: John Wiley and Sons.

Louchakova, O., & Warner, A. (2003). Via Kundalini: Psychosomatic excursions in transpersonal psychology. In *The Humanistic Psychologist*, Ed. Friedman, H., & MacDonald, D. Vol. 31, Numbers 2-3, Spring 2003.

Millon, T. (1981). *Disorders of personality.* New York: John Wiley & Sons.

Moise, E. (1967). *Calculus.* Reading, MA: Addison-Wesley Publishing Company.

Myers, D. (2004). *Psychology.* New York: Worth Publishers.

O'Keefe, J., & Nadel, L. (1978). *The hippocampus as a cognitive map.* Oxford: The Clarendon Press.

Ostander,S., & Schroeder, L. (1970). *Psychic discoveries behind the iron curtain.* NJ: Prentice-Hall.

Ouspensky, P.D. (1981). *Tertium organum.* New York: Vintage Books.

Prophet, E., & Spadaro, P. (2000). *Your seven energy centers.* Corwin Springs, MT: Summit University Press.

Piaget, J. (1976). *The child and reality; Problems of genetic psychology.* New York: Penguin Books.

Pinel, J. (2003). *Biopsychology.* Boston: A and B.

Rodriguez et al. (1999). Perception's shadow: Long distance synchronization of human brain activity. *Nature,* 297, 430-433.

Samples, B. (1976). *The metaphoric mind.* Reading, MA: Addison-Wesley Publishing Company.

Smith, R., & Davis, S. (2003). *The psychologist as detective*. 3rd Ed. New Jersey: Pearson Prentice Hall.

Wilbur, K. (2003). Waves, streams, states, and self: An outline of an integral psychology. In *The Humanistic Psychologist*, Ed. Friedman, H., & MacDonald, D. Vol. 31, Numbers 2-3, Spring 2003.

Winn, R., Editor. (1961). *Psychotherapy in the Soviet Union*. New York: Grove Press.

OTHER BOOKS BY DR. RON DALRYMPLE:

<u>THE INNER MANAGER</u>
Mastering Business, Home and Self
by Dr. Ron Dalrymple

"Profound, the guidebook of a lifetime." ----- The Book Reader

"Imaginative...well-written...plausible." ----- West Coast Review of Books

"Thank-you for sending me this wonderful book."
—- Louise Hay, Best-Selling Author

Seeking a better life for himself and his family, a young man meets a woman executive who takes him on a fascinating journey to his Inner Mind, where he discovers a wealth of talents and powers long hidden beneath his fears and doubts.

In a step-by-step process, he learns he can activate his energy and resources to take a Quantum Leap to a higher level of self- creative thought, offering him virtually unlimited success in life... but it is up to him to make it happen.

He learns how to use the living software of his thoughts to reprogram the hardware of his brain and nervous system, shifting his conscious state and available energy at will.

He discovers the true powers of thought, concentration, will-power, visualization, desire, memory, deductive and inductive reasoning, the infinitizing power of pure love and much more.

He begins to absorb and understand the simple but integrative concepts of Quantum Field Psychology, unveiling the keys to creating a successful life and building a dynamic business.

He learns that by creating his own business or by creating his own niche in his current place of employment, he can take responsibility for his life at a whole new level and truly become the master of his own destiny.

The young man discovers his own Inner Manager, the executive power within his own being always waiting to be called to duty.

8 DAYS TO CREATIVE POWER

Unlock Your Hidden Genius ! by Dr. Ron Dalrymple

Have you ever felt stymied, locked-up inside and unable to truly express yourself? Do you ever feel down on yourself or others, falling into cycles of negative thought and feeling?

"Negative thoughts and feelings," stated Dr. Ron Dalrymple in a recent interview, "greatly limit our ability to solve problems and to attain success and happiness in life."

"By learning how to develop a powerfully positive self-image and by tapping the power of the inner mind, most people can unleash talents and abilities currently dormant inside them."

Dr. Dalrymple's book, originally titled
Increase Your Power of Creative

<u>**Thinking in Eight Days**</u>! (ISBN 0-912057-41-6; LCC No. 85-50428) is based on research conducted at the University of Maryland.

Organized into an eight day program for ease of learning, the book teaches three mind-stimulating approaches to creative thinking.

The first shows you how to tap the power of your vast inner mind and develop a creative self-image.

The second teaches you how to understand problems and the world around you in many new, creative ways.

The third teaches you to put these techniques to practice in your daily life.

A licensed psychologist and creativity expert, Dr. Ron Dalrymple has been a member of the American Psychological Association, numerous

state psychological associations, the National
Register of Health Service Providers in
Psychology, MENSA, Phi Beta Kappa, Phi Kappa
Phi and Psi Chi Honorary Fraternities.

QUANTUM FIELD PSYCHOLOGY

The Thoton Particle Theory
by Dr. Ron Dalrymple

Dr. Ron Dalrymple, a licensed psychologist in multiple states, has developed an integration of modern-day psychologies with quantum physics and topological mathematics known as Quantum Field Psychology.

Quantum Field Psychology starts with the premise that the mind is more than the mere result of the interactions of biochemicals and matter found within the brain, as reductionists and Cartesian thinkers insist.

Dr. Dalrymple works from the theoretical basis that the mind is an energy field that subfuses but transcends the physical brain.

His first premise is that thought energy propagates through space in a wave form, but interacts with matter as a particle.

The smallest unit, or quantum of thought is the thoton (Dalrymple, 1978), just as the photon is the quantum of light.

The second premise of Quantum Field Psychology is that every thought is a form of living software that programs the Superconscious Mind to function in specific ways, affecting not only the hardware of brain and nervous system, but the external world of the individual as well.

This suggests the awesome power of thought when properly trained, focused and concentrated on specific results, especially when powered by intense emotional energy over a period of time.

The third premise of Quantum Field Psychology is that the power of thought can seed an entire universe, and that the first step toward greater mental and planetary health and success in life is to transform all of one's negative thoughts and feelings into positive ones.

Although this sounds elementary, it is most difficult to do.

Try having only positive thoughts and feelings for a month, instantly re-creating all negative thoughts and feelings as soon as they arise.

The fourth premise is that by re-integrating and re-creating one's mind and personality with the techniques of Quantum Field Psychology, the individual can make a series of quantum leaps into universes once beyond her or his imagination.

Dr. Dalrymple's works develop, illustrate and expand upon these premises in simple terms, to help the reader better understand his or her innate human potential in order to master life and become the greatest success one can be.

Dr. Dalrymple offers seminars to corporate, university, professional and multi-level marketing groups on a diversity of topics in the areas of success/motivation, systems analysis, creativity and tapping the power of the Superconscious Mind.

I LOVE YOU, GOD

Proverbs of Peace, Prosperity and Power for the Third Millennium
by Dr. Ron Dalrymple

The purpose of this book is to help the reader focus on Divine ideas every day.

Since what we dwell upon comes upon us, it is important to make a habit of thinking positive, healthy, Divine, inspirational, loving thoughts all day, no matter what other people are doing around us or to us.

One of the greatest difficulties in transforming oneself to a more Divine attitude and perspective is found in working through the negative emotions and beliefs we have long internalized.

These beliefs and emotions become lodged in the subconscious mind, and drive the system automatically until they are changed.

This takes considerable effort and persistence, since the deeply embedded negative emotions tend to link to many different thoughts, attitudes and other feelings.

A virtual labyrinth of interconnected thoughts, emotions and behaviors have to be transformed. This book was created to help the reader achieve that goal.

The intent is for the reader to dwell upon each affirmation of the day with strong feeling, trying to love the very idea being expressed, and projecting it outward to the world.

Each affirmation should be repeated many times throughout the day, and memorized for future use.

As you practice these, your own affirmations will occur to you. Use them all with devotion, because what you worship, is what you become.

<u>**PARADISE FOUND 2015**</u>

A Film Produced
by Dr. Ron Dalrymple

An 18-year-old NASA scientist discovers a new theory of mind that can change the world, and has spent his life in exile proving the theory.

He travels the world to discover the hidden secrets of mind, then labors through graduate school to understand where most psychological systems have failed.

Suppressed and sabotaged by the tyrannical dinosaurs of academic and professional delusion, he finally completes his shocking new theory, Quantum Field Psychology.

He confronts his dying father, a dictatorial CIA agent and World War II veteran experiencing

PTSD with flashbacks to combat, sex-capades in Paris and surreal visions.

The story comes to an explosive conclusion, as the old man arrives at a shocking realization...too late.

Starring Daniel Dasent, Destiny Thomas and James Robert Wood.

A best-selling film on Amazon.com. www.imdbpro.com.

THE ENDLESS QUESTION

A Two Hour Documentary

A Film Written, Produced and Directed by Dr. Ron Dalrymple, Written, best-selling author and award-winning screenwriter and novelist.

Since before time, humankind has pondered one central question...who are we, and why are we here? Many theories have been put forth, by religious leaders, scientists, philosophers, writers, artists and countless others.

None of the theories have held the test of time, because there is a central fact, a hidden truth so powerful it almost transcends comprehension.

It is so shocking, few dare imagine it. To keep this secret question hidden, countless people throughout the centuries have been misled, manipulated, lied to and even slaughtered, their lives ruined to benefit the ruling class.

The most powerful and successful people on earth do not want you to know these truths, because it would undermine their control over the earth's population of sheeple.

Once this incredible truth sweeps the world, nothing will be the same. Don't be left behind on this one.

Watch for...**The Endless Question**.

The Endless Question is a documentary sequel to **Paradise Found 2015** (Amazon), both about **Quantum Field Psychology** (2004), also on Amazon.

Experts, gurus and quantum thinkers from around the world are interviewed by Dr. Ron Dalrymple,

each asked eight key questions about the mind as
an energy field.

Email: drrondal@hotmail.com, or write P.O. Box
4466, N. Ft. Myers, Florida 33918. USA.

CELESTIAL GIFTS PUBLISHING
P.O. Box 4466
N. Ft. Myers, Florida 33918 USA

www.ingramcontent.com/pod-product-compliance
Lightning Source LLC
Chambersburg PA
CBHW061800250726

48657CB00001B/222